THE
PERFECTLY
IMPERFECT
HOME

THE PERFECTLY IMPERFECT HOME

How to Decorate & Live Well

Deborah Needleman

ILLUSTRATIONS BY VIRGINIA JOHNSON

jacqui
small

First published in the UK in 2012 by Jacqui Small LLP
an imprint of Aurum Press Ltd
7 Greenland Street
London NW1 0ND

Published in the United States by Clarkson Potter/Publishers,
an imprint of the Crown Publishing Group, a division of
Random House, Inc., New York.
www.crownpublishing.com
www.clarksonpotter.com

ISBN: 978 1 906417 70 3

A catalogue record for this book is available from the British Library.

2014 2013 2012

10 9 8 7 6 5 4 3 2 1

Printed in China

Book design by Hilary Fitzgibbons
Illustrations by Virginia Johnson
Jacket design by Hilary Fitzgibbons

For Jacob,
Lily, & Nathaniel

CONTENTS

Any house or room
remembered with
pleasure has the look
of being loved by
those who live in it.

—BILLY BALDWIN

INTRODUCTION

Growing up, I was struck by the fact that our house had nothing personal in it. Nobody ever tacked up a picture she found amusing. No memento was brought back from a holiday and put on a shelf. No bunch of flowers was ever cut from the yard and stuck in a vase.

In fact, nothing ever got moved around or changed, until the day the decorators were brought back for an update. There were certain rooms, like the dining room and the living room, that we rarely entered. And there was a piano that no one knew how to play.

It was by no means a sad house. We were loved and cared for, and the house itself was neat and attractive. But I have come to realize that the soul of a house needs attention. Our house had very little life—it wasn't heavily used, engaged with, or loved. It didn't add much to my conception of childhood or happiness.

This led me to appreciate deeply homes that are imbued with a sensibility and spirit—homes with a strong personality and signs of life. It made me long for a home with interesting people and dinner parties and friends spending the night. And it made me dislike homes that look perfect and unlived-in, or that have no whimsy. That is the bias of this book and the reason for writing it.

Embracing imperfection in a home does not mean that anything goes. Here it means aiming for beauty tempered by reality. If real life involves mess, accidents, memory, and the incidental, then so too must decorating account for serendipity, and even embrace it.

The point of decorating, as far as I can tell, is to create the background for the best life you can have. So this book is organized a little bit backwards, starting with what you want your house to do, how you want it to make you feel, and then suggesting furniture or styling tips that may help you get it there. While this is a book about things, I have tried to approach them from the perspective of what these things can offer us.

Decoration can be life-enhancing. It can make dinner parties more fun, kids happier, relaxing easier, talks more intimate, guests at ease. And to think decorating is often considered frivolous. Making a charmed and happy home is a noble endeavor. The simple secret is making sure that every decorating decision

contributes to the creation of beauty and comfort. Beauty to uplift our senses (to transcend the mundane) and comfort to make us feel taken care of (to embrace us in the mundane).

Often, decorators simply impose a style on a client, without regard to location, suitability, or the particulars of that client's life. Yet every decorator in every interview and in every book will profess that he or she prefers a room that feels personal, that money doesn't matter, and that rooms must be comfortable to be chic. Most don't mean it! Why else would there be so many perfectly decorated, perfectly anonymous, entirely expensive, cold rooms filling up the pages of decorating books and magazines? For so many, the "look" is what matters.

Good decoration solves problems elegantly. A stylish home is highly functional and reflects the best possible look for your life, budget, and mode of living (even your peculiarities), and the problems and advantages of the place you live in. This will lead to a home that enhances your sense of well-being, that inspires you and looks after you. Luxury cannot be defined by expense or by grandeur. Style is luxury, and luxury is simply what makes you happy.

What is the goal? A house that is like
the life that goes with it, a house
that gives us beauty as we understand it—
and beauty of a nobler kind
that we may grow to understand.

—ELSIE DE WOLFE

NICE
LIGHTING

I personally try to avoid all ceiling lights because
I think that overhead light is a tragedy.

—ALBERT HADLEY

After college, when I lived in Washington, D.C., I used to love walking around the fancy neighborhood of Georgetown in the evening. I would stare up into the drawing rooms of the town houses, their large, curtain-framed windows aglow with amber warmth. The quality of that light seemed to confer beauty and elegance upon the lives of those inside. I imagined the promise of a Wharton-esque sense of grace and calm: comfortable chairs, a roaring fireplace, fresh flowers, and ice tinkling in well-made drinks.

Back in my apartment, a single bulb held in place by a milky glass globe was the main source of illumination, and it spread its flat, even light grimly around the room. The light was insulting. People look and feel better emerging from light, not bathed in it. Or in the words of decorator Kathryn Ireland, "Ask any woman to name one overhead light she considers her ally."

This image of a house at night, glowing from within, has always remained in my mind. While those Georgetown manses were as likely to be filled with bitter alcoholics as they were with gracious laughter, light absolutely does affect how we feel and, to some extent, how we behave. Consider good lighting to be a prerequisite to style. Without it, a place won't ever have a pleasing atmosphere, regardless of how fantastic all your stuff might be.

Previous pages: The living room in Steven Gambrel's New York City town house has a variety of lighting sources that create a warm glow.

Beautiful rooms tend to have soft pools of light that come from a variety of sources. The goal is to create a sense of depth, seducing the eye with highlights and lowlights. Lamps, according to decorator Billy Baldwin, "decorate a room with light," and different kinds do so in different ways.

Dealing with Cords
Minimize the visual
annoyance of plugs
and wires by painting
your socket to match
the wall. Buy a light-
or dark-hued plug to
match (or paint it to
match), or have lamps
wired with inoffensive
clear or fabric cords.

Table Lamps

To my mind, nothing beats old-fashioned lamps for their quality of light. By "old-fashioned" I mean those still modeled directly after their candle and oil lamp predecessors—in the shape of an urn or a candlestick—with a lampshade stuck on top like a hat. While there are, of course, many cooler, more designer-y lamps, most don't manage to create a more winning light, only perhaps a more novel shape.

Many lamps are still made, as they've always been, from terra-cotta jars, glass bottles, Chinese urns, or old silver candlesticks. And you can always take an item you love and have it wired into a lamp.

Table lamps are really such excellent decorating tools, it would be tempting to use them even if they did nothing. They are strong verticals in the sea of horizontal furniture that is most rooms. Plus, they make for a wonderful starting point for decorating on a table.

STYLE TIP
When you have
overnight guests,
switch on a lamp in
their room at dusk
so they won't enter
into darkness.

STYLE TIP
A lamp is the perfect
decorating starting
point for objects
on a table. Take your
cues from its style,
color, or material
to arrange a pleasing
tableau of things
around it.

A gay friend once exclaimed in horror that my bedside lighting was terribly "heterosexual"! What he meant was how unromantic and bright it was. True, the lamp was loaded up with a pair of 75-watt bulbs—optimal for reading, but a bit much for love. Ah, but therein lies the beauty of the double-bulb lamp! One bulb can be 60 watts and one 40. Together they're a powerhouse duo, but on their own, you have both a medium and a low setting.

Put It Here: Table Lamp

There are very few spots in a home that don't benefit from the lovely light of a table lamp.

- Front hall console (so warm and welcoming)
- Side tables (next to sofas and chairs)
- Tables behind sofas (a pair here can be nice)
- Bedside tables (mismatched works!)
- Dressers (especially in front of a mirror)
- Mantel (a skinny lamp is good)
- Ledge of a bookshelf (small, again)
- Drinks table (lights up the bottles and glasses)
- Kitchen counter (very homey)
- A shelf or ledge in the bathroom (to prevent a too-bathroomy feel)

Fitting a Shade Sorry, but you have to drag the whole lamp into the shade store and try on shades like outfits to see which looks best. It is next to impossible to eyeball it, even for pros.

Lampshade Literacy

The quality of light is affected by the material and shape of the lampshade.

Paper Shades
- Least expensive
- Translucent versions glow when the lamp is on
- Parchment-colored paper creates warmth; in white they feel more modern and the light is cooler

Fabric Shades
- Create the warmest, most glamorous light
- Can be custom-made with any textile
- Fabric can be laid flat or shirred
- Add decorative pattern, intrigue, and a layered dimension to a room, even when the light is off
- Silks tend toward an uptown traditional feel, while linen, cotton, and printed fabric swing more Bohemian
- Line them in a tobacco or blush color, not white

Opacity
- Opaque shades are more dramatic (especially in black), as they throw light up and down (without allowing any to spill through the sides)
- Opaque insides, whether fabric or paper, can be tinted; Billy Baldwin preferred face-flattering pink, while Mark Hampton went for the sparkly glamour of gold foil

Shape
- The most gracious shape flares out at a slight angle from top to bottom
- Straight sides look modern and sleek (they emit equal amounts of light up as down—and for me, down is where I want it to go)
- A nipped and flaring waistline looks girly and Victorian

Floor Lamps

Floor Lamps Standing lamps get a bit of an unfair rap because their proportions can be rather gangly. But don't dismiss them out of hand, because they are wonderful for providing variety and height, and can prove useful beside a reading chair, where their light is closer and more direct than their tabletop cousin's could ever be. The most effective lamps for reading are task lamps with adjustable arms and small shades, particularly those with tented metal shades that throw the light down just where you need it. These lamps often have a sort of nineteenth-century industrial look that can break up the softness of upholstery with a little hard edge.

In an ideal world, you would plot out where all your furniture and lamps would go before you moved in, then put sockets just where you need them, including in the floor. Those of us not living in an ideal world can actually cut a tiny slit in the rug and thread the wire through and under it. If this seems outrageous or makes you angry, then forget I said it. But know that decorators do this all the time.

Reading Nook Essentials

- **Armchair:** In the main seating area or off on its own, populating an otherwise empty corner
- **Side Table:** At arm height or lower
- **Reading Light:** A lamp with focused illumination works best
- **Footrest:** Anything you can put your feet on, from a little stool or ottoman to a corner of the coffee table (yes, feet belong on the furniture!)

STYLE TIP
Consider putting
mounted fixtures
at the top of
bookshelves or above
a painting. The
soft lowlights from
these add depth
to a room like
nobody's business.

Sconces There are two distinct kinds: those that extend out from the wall, often topped with a fabric or metal shade, and the flatter, sconcier sconces that lay flush to the wall and are the electrified descendants of mounted candleholders.

The extended-arm wall lights are for spot lighting and are typically used when furniture is pushed up against a wall and there is no room for a proper lamp. This is why you often find them behind a bed or above a banquette, or in a small hallway on either side of a mirror, saving precious tabletop space. In a bedroom or bathroom, where clarity is key, the shades are usually white or ivory, but in a living room or a powder room, a colored shade adds warmth and richness to the light and some extra personality to the room. Many decorators outfit canopied beds with both swing-arm fixtures for polite, individual reading and table lamps for ambience.

The flatter, sconcier sconces are accent lights that provide an opportunity for whimsy and a bit of sparkle—especially when they are mounted on mirrored backs, as many are. If you are lucky enough to have a fireplace, you can't go wrong with sconces above the mantel on either side. And if you have a mirror above the fireplace, try to place the sconces so they reflect in it. There is, however, no law of pairs, and a single sconce can be like a work of art, whether hung alone or mingled with pictures and mirrors in an artful, assymetrical jumble.

• Don't allow your main
light source to be an
overhead fixture—
what my college
roommate referred
to as the "dread
overhead."
• Position lights all
around the room to
avoid dark corners.
• Layer a variety
of fixtures: a hanging
light, sconces,
bookshelf lights,
table lamps, etc.

Hanging Lights

Hanging fixtures come in a multitude of appealing forms—lantern, pendant, orb, chandelier—and increasingly interesting materials like glass, fabric, ceramic, metal, paper, and shell. Each offers style and punctuation in addition to light. Like a rug, a hanging lamp helps to define an area and can lend a sense of focus to a space, like a dining room or a seating arrangement.

Here too there are the taskier lamps, like pendant fixtures, that throw light downward, which is always good over a counter or a table, and then there are the more decorative ones, like chandeliers, that play with light in various ways. In neither case should hanging lights be forced to do all the heavy lifting. I was at a dinner party recently where a gorgeous Venetian glass chandelier above the table shone on us; it made the area seem like an interrogation chamber. Hanging lights (like all overheads) are co-conspirators, not lone gunmen. They are not the place for your highest-watt bulbs. Instead, an overhead fixture needs to spread light a bit more softly. Even if you're in a rental, replacing the mean overhead fixture with something gentler, if only an expensive paper lantern, will make a world of difference.

STYLE TIP
Ambience's best
friend is a dimmer
switch: put
these on all lights,
but especially
recessed ones.

A
PROPER
WELCOME

First impressions may be wrong
but they are nevertheless important.

— DAVID HICKS

The hallway has a tougher task than most rooms. It needs to set the tone for our home and at the same time accommodate all the junk we drag in. The idea is to get the hallway to act as the butler we don't have—greeting us and our visitors graciously, whisking away our coats, bags, and parcels, and then offering those things when we need to go out again.

As the public face of our private realm, the front hall should present a sense of order and graciousness, both for our friends, who will be ushered through, and for the delivery guy, who will remain on its threshold.

Sadly, this quaint ambition has nothing to do with my personal reality, in which the hallway is likely filled with the scent of playground and littered with soiled socks and shoes and piles of unopened mail. Fortunately, decorating is about trying to bring our desires in line with our reality.

Our basic tools in this mission (or struggle) are hooks and hangers, a table, some lights, a mirror, and a chair or bench. But what kind we choose depends on who we are and how and where we live. The mantra of Elsie de Wolfe, the self-proclaimed inventor of the decorating profession, was "Suitability, suitability, suitability!" There is a reason we use wicker furniture, cotton fabrics, and stone floors in hot climates, and wool and wood, velvet and leather in cold ones. Likewise, regardless of how much you adore the frippery of spindly French antiques and fragile porcelain objets, they might not be just the thing in the cramped apartment you share with an excitable dog and a full-size husband.

Previous pages: The front hall of Kate and Andy Spade's New York City apartment, which has every gracious amenity—lovely light, plenty of storage, a mirror, and a place to sit.

STYLE TIP
You can exaggerate the mood in a hallway. As a pass-through, it can handle boldly patterned wallpaper or a bright, unexpected color— things that might drive you around the bend in a sitting room or bedroom.

A Primping Place As much as we want bright lights and clear mirrors in which to see ourselves, you may also want to create a mood, and few things offer up more elegance than an antique mirror or some soft lighting. Sconces, in addition to saving space, cast a rather romantic glare. Hanging lanterns, particularly glass ones, are traditional in hallways, feeling as they do like a cross between an outdoor light and an indoor one. (Make sure that the main illumination is not behind you when you're looking in the mirror.)

A table with a small pencil drawer comes in very handy for notepads, spare change, and leashes. If you are short on closet space, go for a dresser that can hold all your out-the-door necessities, like gloves and scarves. If you are lucky enough to have a true entry room (as opposed to a passageway or a stair hallway), nothing looks better than a big round table with a great lantern hanging over it. A round hallway table also gives you another place to have dinners or serve drinks at big cocktail parties. But your primping station may also just be a shelf with a mirror above it and a clip-on light attached to it. It's not the size that counts, it's the accessories you use.

Think of Suitability as a Mathematical Equation
Suitability = How you live +
what you want + where you live

History Lesson

In the eighteenth century, a hallway was designed to be as tranquil and restful as possible in order to soothe arriving guests after what was almost always a long and difficult journey. This sense of calm came from the austerity of the architecture, the paucity of furnishings, and the bare floors. The effect may have been a little cold, but that must've made it especially wonderful to then be ushered into a cozy sitting room with a nice fire going, given a warm drink, and doted on for news of the world. The hallway should still be thought of as a transitional space. While we don't want it to seem cold, neither do we want to bombard ourselves or our visitors with the details and detritus of our lives.

A Modern-Day Conundrum

Many houses have an entry space that will accommodate a beautiful round center hall table with a lantern hanging above it—the most classic and splendid hallway setup. But often, no one passes through it; they trudge in through the kitchen instead. On special occasions (dinner parties, holidays, etc.), encourage guests to use the front door by setting some lanterns along the path and on the front steps. When you hear guests pull up, greet them from the front door. And voilà, there will be jolly people in your beautiful front hall!

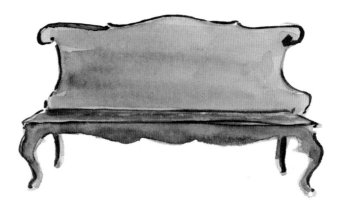

A Spot to Sit

Having a comfortable place to sit while putting on shoes is very civilized and adds to the "roomness" of this passageway. A seat can be anything from a little bench to a couple of antique settees. If you don't have much room, consider a small bench or two that can slide under the console, which looks layered and very chic. (It's nice to fill in those empty areas under tables.) In a narrow stair hallway, it's customary to flank a console or a dresser with a pair of chairs, and inevitably one gets used as a landing spot for bags or books.

Bins, Bowls, and Baskets

Quite simply, the more designated places you have for specific items, the less your hallway will end up resembling a junkyard or a branch of the post office. Making a spot for your keys, sunglasses, cell phones, and mail is an opportunity to accessorize the space with appealing bowls, baskets, boxes, or trays. (A shopportunity, in fact!) Trays are miracle workers, transforming random junk into seemingly organized groupings. Even in an apartment with no real hallway, these containers can be stashed on nearby shelves.

Hooks, Hangers, and Hampers

The more storage a person has, the happier that person is going to be. Is anyone's coat closet ever large enough? The answer is almost always no. But you can maximize your space. Matching hangers (in wood, please) allow you to fit more, and they look neat. Baskets on shelves (separated by household member) are great for stowing hats, gloves, and miscellany. And hooks, especially on the inside of the closet door, are great for incentivizing the young as well as the lazy.

Not everything need be hidden, however. A lively sense of functionality comes from corralling coats, hats, and sports equipment into useful clusters with hooks and baskets out where you can get to the items easily.

I am crazy for those great English country houses with their beautiful hall furniture covered with old tennis racquets and flower trugs and dog leashes and other signs of outdoorsiness. Hockey sticks and baseball bats poking out of buckets make a house feel homey and lived-in. A bit of the country-house look can work well in the city too, even if only for umbrellas or hats and scarves.

Similarly, the look in photo spreads of hats, jackets, and totes hanging at the ready with garden boots beneath them on the floor is compelling. To pull it off, though, I find that some big baskets (and a closet) are necessary to hide the more unsightly things. Which brings us back to the point that the more storage one has, the happier one is!

Try These

Use these containers to translate the supplies-left-out country-house look wherever you are:

- A giant urn
- Heavy old ceramic vases
- Umbrella stands
- Open hampers
- Tall glass vases
- Tin buckets
- Log baskets
- Antique picnic baskets

PLACES
FOR
CHATTING

A comfortable chair is the most
hospitable piece of furniture one can own.

—CHARLOTTE MOSS

f one third of our lives is spent in bed, then much of the other two thirds must be spent with our bottoms in a seat. This means that sofas and chairs may be the most important pieces of furniture in our repertoire.

A variety of chair types and a companionable furniture arrangement are essential to decorating for happy times. What kind of chairs you have and how you arrange them can encourage anything from an intimate gossip or a kicked-back, feet-up after-dinner conversation to lively party chatter or quiet reading. Some chairs beckon us to sprawl, while others make us feel protected and supported, and still others are just the thing for pulling up to join a conversation in progress. The goal is to have a mix of options and to lay them out in a way that is well-considered but not so perfectly "done" that it looks uptight and suppresses spontaneity. If guests tend to stand around uncomfortably instead of sitting, or are afraid to pull a chair up to the sofa or move a cushion, I don't think the house can be called stylish.

Keep in mind that furniture is not bolted to the floor; real life requires a bit of flexibility. As with many things—from creating outfits to doing your hair—sometimes messing it up a little is just the thing!

Previous pages: The Paris living room of Matilde Agostinelli, decorated by Jacques Grange, features a pair of plump armchairs and a lightweight chair that can be moved about as needed.

A Deep and Cozy Armchair (or Two) The implicit promise of upholstered furniture is pleasure and comfort, and every home needs a few chairs that just beg to be sat in. The range of possibilities here is endless—from curvy, ruffle-skirted seats to the leather cubes of Corbusier to the overstuffed delight of the English armchair. What all of these should have in common is ample butt room, some nice padding, a sloping back, and a comfortable disposition of the armrests.

The decorating guru Billy Baldwin rightly considered upholstered chairs to be the backbone of a room. They work well as a matching pair sitting side by side—either angled slightly toward each other or neatly parallel—or facing each other across a coffee table. Around them and in relation to them, secondary seating can be arranged more loosely.

History Lesson

Until the seventeenth century, seats were hard, sturdy, upright things that were moved about as needed. Even as their backs began to be upholstered, chairs were still kept lined up along the walls when not in use. The idea of a stable furniture arrangement is a twentieth-century concept. It was in the court of Louis XV that the upholstered seat softened further, loosening its ramrod posture into a gently sloping back and opening out into a more capacious girth. This innovation was the "bergère," the first chair built for the purpose of comfort, and a shape still popular today. The seventeenth-century ladies of the Marquise de Rambouillet's salon referred to bergères quite aptly (and adorably) as "the indispensables of conversation."

An Upright Chair

In your mix of upholstered chairs, it's nice to have one or two that are taller and firmer than a deep armchair. Older people tend to gravitate toward these because they can get up from them more easily. And sometimes you don't want to fall back into a chair, but just to sit upright on one. For those who like a more tailored or formal look in their sitting rooms, a pair of upholstered upright chairs might replace deep armchairs.

The other nice thing about upright chairs is the visual variety they introduce. You don't want your living room to look like a fat upholstery party. Often showing a little leg or wood frame, these more stand-up seats offer a break from sofas and deep armchairs, which are usually entirely swathed in fabric. This is precisely what John Fowler was describing when he tried to explain the magic of Colefax and Fowler's English country house style: "English furniture, all foursquare and sensible, was relieved by the delicacy of a French piece."

Options for modern upright pieces abound, but the striking silhouette of an English or American wing chair or a French bergère or fauteuil is great. If you choose an antique, make sure it is sturdy and not spindly so that you don't sacrifice the sense of security that comes from being able to lean back and feel protected.

Style Cheat Sheet
2 deep chairs + 1 upright = Cozy room
2 upright chairs + 1 deep = Formal room

A Really Good Sofa Sofas may be the most emotionally loaded furniture in our homes: they are costly and massive and have an impact on everything else in a room. Their basic design hasn't changed a whole lot in the past hundred years; most are just variations on classic shapes. To choose one that is right for you, it helps to get a sense of their differences.

The one rule-ish thing I will suggest is to not cheap out in the upholstered furniture department. After years of buying "placeholder" sofas because I felt I couldn't afford a quality one, I've learned that the sofa is the place to spend as much as you possibly can. A quality sofa lasts a lifetime.

Many cheap catalog sofas are steroidally overscaled, bulky, and inelegant. But more important, they're less well made and will wear out and end up in a landfill long before a high-quality or custom sofa will. (I'm not going to bore you with details on craftsmanship, eight-way hand-tying, and corner joints, so just trust me.)

Quality translates into beauty and comfort. When was the last time you sunk into or were enveloped by a solid block of foam? That's what's inside a cheap sofa. The ideal stuffing is soft down (for some give), perhaps wrapped around a thin piece of foam for some shape-holding stability. Next time you see a piece of upholstery, check out the line of the cushions. On a high-quality sofa, the line will look like it was drawn by hand rather than like the razor-straight line of a machine indicating a hunk of foam.

The book *Mark Hampton on Decorating* shows the family sofa in its original incarnation as a centerpiece for their David Hicks–designed 1960s mod plexi-and-chrome pad through its second life in the 1970s, reupholstered in chintz to blend seamlessly with Mark's developing signature style. This same sofa stayed with Mark and his wife, Duane, from that first tiny apartment as a young married couple through the upbringing of their children, through their lives as empty nesters. It now resides—forty-odd years on—in Duane's rather feminine apartment. Case closed.

Basic Sofas Styles, with Benefits

Slipper

Armless. The longer cousin of the slipper chair (whose defining feature was upholstery covering all wood parts so women could slip on their stockings without snagging them). Benefits: Fits in small spaces. Good for seating a group of people. Even if cushions look loose, they are usually built in so they don't slip off.

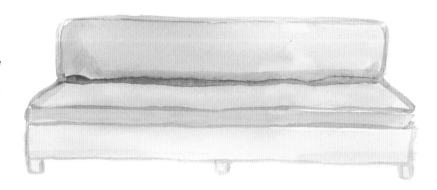

Chesterfield

A tailored look from the 1920s. Tufted with rolled arms and back of the same height. Benefits: Chic detailing counteracts some of the typical blobbiness of sofas; high sides encourage intimate chats. When clad in leather, looks clubby; when in velvet, looks elegant.

Odd, but True Regardless of how big your sofa is, it's rare that more than three people will sit together on it.

English

Classic 1820s-era English sofa. Very low and deep seat with loose seat cushions and an upholstered back.
Benefits: Ideal for vegging out and for chats with your legs curled up under you. Has a rumpled, casual look.

Bridgewater

The most casual of looks, with low, softly rolled arms and a high back. Usually has a skirt, and loose seat and back cushions.
Benefits: Comfortable, with easy-to-clean slipcovered cushions.

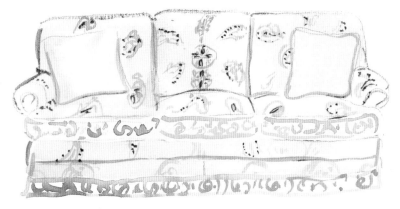

Tuxedo

Named for the fancy town Tuxedo Park in New York. High straight arms and back of the same height. Cushions usually all loose. It was Billy Baldwin's favorite sofa, and any streamlined modern sofas descend from it.
Benefits: Can easily swing modern or traditional, and looks good with a mix of both. Remove the back cushions and you've got a nice spare bed.

Best not to cover
your sofa with that
personality-expressing
statement fabric you've
been eyeing. You
know, the one with
the giant Marimekko
flowers. Not only will
you probably tire
of it quickly, but it also
limits your choices
for the rest of the
room. Save the super
bold for the smaller
pieces, like armchairs,
cushions, and throws.
As Billy Baldwin
observed, "Large,
immovable furniture
should be quietly
permanent, [but]
'floating' chairs can
be as brilliant as
one wishes."

Little Sofas

As long as you've got your comfortable sofa, it's nice to have a second sofa—or settee, really—that is weighted perhaps more toward style than substance. A beautiful wood-framed, leggy sofa in the French or Swedish style or a camel-back or Sheraton-style settee serves as a great counterpoint in a living room that already has a large couch.

Settees can also be useful for filling an empty space in a room or wedging into a tight one such as on a stair landing or in an odd nook. I know this seems counterintuitive to my insistence on how we must use our things, but sometimes just the thought or vision of repose is pleasing, even if you never actually sit there. Better than a naked niche or a decorating bald spot!

Stools and Benches

Stools and benches, whether upholstered or not, are just the kind of versatile pieces I love. These little perches—which can be anything from upholstered benches whose legs cross in an "x" to Barcelona stools to Moroccan poufs or African stools—have much to recommend them as extra seating. Because you can see straight over them, they seem to disappear instead of cluttering up a room or blocking the view. Used in pairs—for instance on the other side of the coffee table from the sofa—they are like the punctuation that completes a conversational grouping. Another genius feature: you can stow them under a table or console. This tried-and-true decorator trick fills up the leggy undersides beneath tables and consoles, adding a nice layered effect while blocking any negative space. You can even employ these little seats as occasional tables in a pinch. Our furniture should strive to be as versatile as our rooms!

A Very Bossy Primer on Furniture Arranging

Get your furniture off the wall.
A big mistake beginners make is putting all the furniture against the walls, encircling the room. To encourage conversation, move your big pieces (sofa, armchairs) into the center of the room. (This will also make the space seem larger!)

Enjoy your new real estate. With your furniture pulled into the center of the room, you've opened up space along the walls for all the other pieces that make a room worth hanging out in—a reading chair, a games table, or a console topped with books, flowers, and artwork.

Don't make me say this. Please do not get a matching set of furniture. Your armchairs should not be the same as your sofa. Matchy-matchy equals no point of view—the cardinal sin.
Say yes to symmetry. Armchairs, lamps, and side tables can be nice as matched pairs, bringing a sense of cohesion and calm to a room.

A Spare Chair This is a chair-in-waiting, residing on the outskirts of your furniture arrangement or your room. It's not a "go-to" chair, so much as an "and also" chair. Perfect helpers for preventing a static layout, these chairs create the dynamism necessary to a lively, lived-in space. The main attribute of the spare is that it is lightweight and easily moved. (Thus, it is usually armless and often made of wood.)

While you want your living room to be able to accommodate a lot of people when you need it to, you don't want it to look like a chair convention 24/7. A pair of spares quietly flanking a fireplace or around a console can easily be pulled from sentinel duty. (And in fact, seats by the fire are often the first ones taken by guests even if they are the least comfy.)

Spare chairs can also be a regular, yet mobile, part of your furniture arrangement. If you have two furniture groupings, these seats can be turned to face one group or another. Like its cousin the odd chair (see page 70), spare chairs can perform in the "interesting-as-sculpture" category, but the difference is that their main purpose is function more than form.

Say no to symmetry. You don't want too much of a good thing: OD'ing on symmetry makes a room dull and stiff. Throw things off a bit with some single chairs of a different shape or style, like a wing chair.

Arrange chairs so they "talk." Not everything around the coffee table should be at right angles. Like people, chairs want to "look" at one another.

Don't get stuck. It is wise to start with a furniture plan before you shop, but don't be afraid to rearrange, and then rearrange again and again. This is often the only way to find the ideal solution. Plus, your same old things can look completely different when reshuffled.

Build in flexibility. Big pieces like sofas and heavy chairs can't be moved around every time you want to scoot closer to someone or accommodate extra people. Lightweight chairs or benches can, and they loosen up an otherwise static arrangement.

A BIT
OF
QUIRK

I prefer an ugly, personal room to one that is just
cold and correct—a mausoleum done by a decorator.

—BILLY BALDWIN

An element of quirkiness in your decor shows that you do not take decorating or, by extension, yourself too seriously. A room that is decorated within an inch of its life feels self-important and static. Style ought to be loose and easygoing; capacious and expansive! A little something unexpected makes us comfortable. Quirkiness and its side-kick, charm, represent the lighthearted humanity of your home.

To say that a home should feel light, and have a sense of wit or whimsy about it, is not to say that a house should be "fun" or goofy. (Kooky is fine for people, but not for decor.) When everything in a room has provenance or is absolutely just so, that room fails to put you at ease and welcome you and then, well, what is the point? I have seen rooms by decorators that are so gorgeous they are like visual poetry. Yet usually they are not livable—only gorgeous, only perfect. They are rooms without spirit, without serendipity, without potential for amusement. Sad. Sad. Sad. A bit of humor, a touch of fantasy, or even something haphazard feels welcoming. It invites us to let our guard down. Quirk is less about shopping or objects and more about attitude. Quirk humanizes.

Previous pages: In a room decorated by Johnson Hartig, nothing is too perfect: unmatched cushions sit on a loosely slipcovered sofa; shelves are stocked with bar essentials and hung with an old mirror and tiny framed pictures. In fact, it's perfect.

Irreverent Accents These are small, whimsical touches that show you don't take the objects in your home too seriously: snapshots stuck into the edge of a beautiful antique mirror, a hat atop a formal bust, a beaded necklace hanging from a lampshade. Putting things where they aren't "supposed" to be shows that you rule your roost and not the other way around. Framed pictures leaning against the wall or against a mirror show that the house is dynamic, alive, a work in progress. Rita Konig, my friend and patron saint of quirk and style, tapes Polaroids of her friends on her living room wall in an ever-growing collection. She also hangs her coat and hat on a standing lamp in her front hall because she is short on closet space.

In really grand English country houses there always seems to be a lampshade askew, especially in photo shoots, making me wonder if Lord Who-ever tipped it slightly before the shutter snapped so it wouldn't look like he cared too much. Whatever the truth, the trick is not to care so much that you can't make space for the silly or the sweet. My irrepressibly loquacious friend Maria came upon a note she was forced to write as a child in school: "I will not talk in school. I will not talk in school. . . ." She framed it and hung it on the wall. It is deeply personal, and also hilarious.

Jollifiers Jollifiers are sentimental things that spread a little joy every time you cast your eye upon them. They are among the easiest decorating tools, as they require no skill, no complicated understanding of color, texture, or composition. You basically set them out and, like a talisman, they exude their subtle power. Rita has a big poster with the word LOVE on it, and every time my eyes brush over it I feel some tiny, almost imperceptible lift in my mood. When she first moved to New York from London, the poster was one of the few things she took with her. For a while, it was almost the only decoration in her new apartment. Somehow it made the empty apartment (and probably the brave, uprooted girl who lived there) seem less lonely.

Rita loves to dress beds with Porthault's heart-covered sheets and shams, so that the beds themselves seem like big happy things eager to have you join them. I find polka dots very jolly. Anything spotted is slightly silly and friendly.

Among my favorite jollifiers is a collection of ceramic pieces I found in the basement of my husband's childhood home: they were from a one-man show he had in the school hallway in sixth grade. The collection includes a Crest tube oozing paste, a whale spouting water, and a glazed doughnut that opens like a box. The pieces occupy a shelf in a gray-painted Swedish bookcase atop a few stacks of books. Their shiny surfaces are a nice, happy counterpoint to the soft wood.

Pictures by Children The art of children (and their notes and doodles) is really a subcategory of jollifier. A little goes a long way, but children's expressionistic scrawls are nothing if not joyful and quirky. Small children are like in-house artists—very easy to commission by subject or occasion. You can often just hand them crayons and ask for a flower portrait. I once saw a Twombly-esque framed scribble that fit perfectly above the fireplace where it was hung. I later found out that the child had been given the exact size paper on which to work his magic. Pulling out one or two special pictures and mixing them in with real art, or giving a good place or a nice frame to a child's drawing, shows a sweet insouciance.

Mollifiers Mollifiers, well, mollify. This is the stuff that you allow into your home because as awful as it may be, it makes someone else happy. Each person's list varies. Items could include, for instance, noisy plastic weapons (my son), posters of sluttily clad tweens ripped from fan magazines and tacked onto the wall (my daughter), and a collection of framed anarchist posters from the Spanish Civil War (my husband). There is a softening of attitude that comes from allowing some of these things into your life.

A famous example of decorating mollification is Jackie Kennedy's acceptance of President Kennedy's goofy rocking chair in the yellow Oval Room of the White House. She thought the chair ugly, vowing to the decorator Sister Parish that they'd get it out of there somehow. But it was her husband's beloved ugly thing. So in a drawing room filled with Louis XVI furniture, this bit of Americana remained and was where Kennedy sat when receiving heads of state. And in truth, it chic-ed up the room by being so quirky and unexpected.

I'm not saying some fake leather recliner chair should get any play in the house, but it's good to allow a little flexibility for what has significance for others. A really chic person can mollify because she puts love before style—and she can look upon the offending items as amusing, or at least as part of the package.

Some Small Animals

I am not even going to venture a guess as to why—other than to say that people like cute things and animals are cute—it is so nice to have a small creature in figurine form here and there in your house among your things. A funny stuffed animal on a nicely made bed, a white porcelain monkey on your dining table, a painted Staffordshire dog in your bookshelf, a nutcracker in the shape of a schnauzer, or a big gold piggy bank on your mantel. Don't question me here, just pick up a nice, inanimate pet along your journeys, bring it home, and see how you feel.

An Odd Chair

This useful chair is not primarily for sitting. Desirable for its amusing demeanor, it is more like a piece of sculpture in the shape of a chair. Of all furniture types, chairs probably have the most personality—they often feel a little human, standing on four legs with outstretched arms as they do. In the world of chairs, the odd chair is the most individual of all. It is often diminutive, unusual-looking, and solitary. Sister Parish called these "personality" chairs, and insisted every room should have one. In addition to adding quirk, the odd chair can hold a stack of books or an ashtray, a bunch of flowers or a lamp. It often acts more like a little occasional table than like a chair.

Some Odd Chairs

- A funny Victorian piece that would overwhelm if it were part of a set but instead grins like a Cheshire cat from the sidelines of the room
- A child's chair pulled up in front of the coffee table
- A Gothic-style wood chair in front of a bookcase, holding overflow
- A bistro chair acting as a magazine stand

If you have pieces that feel a little too off, transform them with some fabric or a can of paint. Many people feel it is sacrilegious to cover wood with paint, but I'm not one of them. Unless it is some fine eighteenth-century wood, better just to bring the piece in line with the way you live than to let it sit there looking dreary and hinting at the Dumpster.

Accidental Furniture Even if you think you're done decorating, you are not. (Sorry, but you're never really done.) You always need to leave space for what may happen, for the happy accidents of a well-lived life.

Accidental furniture pieces are those things that just happen to attach themselves to you—things you never meant to acquire and maybe don't even love. But there they are, and there they have been, with you for quite some time. In their imperfection or randomness, they are companionable. They carry memories, tell a little story of your past. An accidental piece may be a dresser from childhood that you brought with you to college, or a table a friend "loaned" you because you had space for it when he didn't.

I have a set of rather ugly, straight-sided, gold-rimmed coffee cups—they can't seem to decide if they want to be modern or fancy—that belonged to my grandmother. My husband takes his coffee from one every morning. And in their ugliness, they are really kind of dear, drawing a line between Nana Tillie and my husband, who never met her.

Something Unexpected

Every home needs something a little surprising to lift it out of the mundane. Delight can be found by defying expectations—but it is not as simple as just introducing some wackadoodle color in the bathroom or a giant urn into your living room and letting it shout "Surprise!" like a jack-in-the-box. The unexpected element must form a relationship with other things in the room, and also be given space to "breathe." For a surprise to be sophisticated and not jokey, we need to achieve a balance between things, which in truth is not so easy to do.

For instance, a picture hung below eye level—what is considered too low—can be an unusual, pleasing detail if there is something like a seat or a table adjacent that it relates to. Otherwise, it would look more like an irritating mistake, and you would want to return it to its "right" place.

Similarly, if you set an ornate chandelier over a plain, rustic table, its impact is greater than if it were hanging over an equally ornate table. In fact, the impact of each piece is enhanced—you feel more keenly the simple table *and* the elaborate fixture. David Hicks loved to put tiny bouquets under really large paintings or giant ones next to tiny pictures.

In Nathalie and Amir Farman-Farma's high-ceilinged sitting room, a giant palm tree in a terra-cotta pot towers over the furniture, all of which is quite low. The ground-hugging furniture actually enhances the super verticality of the plant and the height of the room. And the tree's singularity makes the room seem majestic.

Ways to Surprise

- Art where it doesn't "belong," like hung really low
- A big shift in scale, like a giant painting or urn
- Color where you don't expect it, such as inside a closet or on a ceiling
- Mixing two opposing styles, say, minimalist and rococo
- Hanging one of your better pictures in the powder room

Creating Color Continuity

Take one room's wall color and carry it into the next room with objects and fabrics. So, a pink-walled hallway leads into a room with, say, a pink vase or cashmere throw. Not only does this create a visual flow, but it also gives you an emotional flow—your home is connected room by room in a vital way.

SPOTS
FOR BOOKS,
DRINKS,
& FEET

No room can be called
perfect unless it has real comfort.

—DOROTHY DRAPER

W e've got places to sit, but now we need a nice place for our books, bevs, and feet. In other words, it's time to accessorize our seating. A chair needs an occasional table, a sofa needs an end table, drinks require a coffee table, and everyone likes a little ottoman or something on which to rest his feet. These pieces allow our rooms to live up to their gracious potential. And best of all, many of these pieces can do double duty.

Previous pages:
A sitting room by Peter Dunham with a small table near every chair.

Ottomans I adore furniture that is versatile. I am not talking about tricky furniture like beds that fold up and turn into tables or workstations that become TV stands. I'm talking about simple, elegant furniture that seems singular in purpose, and yet affords oh-so-many options and possibilities. The ottoman is the ultimate example: coffee table, footstool, and seating all in one. It is whatever you want whenever you want it. (If only people were so flexible and accommodating.)

In the center of a furniture arrangement, these flat slabs of upholstery on legs can provide a comfortable home for multiple pairs of feet, chic piles of coffee-table books, and useful trays topped with bouquets of flowers, drinks, and anything else a lazy lounger might desire. Having a party? Edit down what's on top, or move things to one side so people can populate the ottoman's perimeters to chat amiably (or not) with others sitting in chairs.

Ottoman Types
- A small square (that can hold a single tray)
- An unusual form (like clover-shaped)
- A large, room-grounding octagon
- A long rectangle large enough to provide foot support for everyone on the sofa
- A diminutive footstool

Coffee Tables

This serviceable table sits in front of the sofa, providing a place for all the little things we need—or just like to look at. Hailing from the 1920s, the coffee table, with its long, low-slung profile, has the glamorous feel of its flapper-era origins, when it was created to hold cocktails (hence its other moniker, the cocktail table), as well as ashtrays, cigarette cases, and lighters. (It created its own chief accessory: the coffee-table book.)

A coffee table, no matter how fancy or fine, is a relaxed piece of furniture residing only about fifteen inches off the ground that can really be fashioned out of anything we want: an ottoman (as we discussed), a pair of smallish tables or upholstered stools, or even an old steamer trunk. All of which provide excellent opportunities for styling. Choose what you use—books, magazines, boxes, candles, trays, flowers, objects, etc.—according to what pleases your eye. The useful should be tempered by the beautiful here, and the beautiful ought to be useful. And if it comes down to a relaxed evening at home, you can sweep it all to the side and kick your feet up.

Occasional Tables These small-scale, low tables can go where you need them. Every chair should really have an uncluttered table next to it for setting down things like drinks and books and gadgets. (Putting stuff on the floor is just asking for trouble.) When a coffee table or an end table is busy with lamps and trays and such, these versatile little guys can be called in as backup to handle the overflow. Use them next to a larger table or simply pulled up near a chair or a sofa. Not only practical, occasional tables also create a warm, layered look that is intriguing. Often these small, easily moved-about tables hail from exotic locales like Morocco or Eygpt and have lovely detailing, like Moorish carving or inlaid designs.

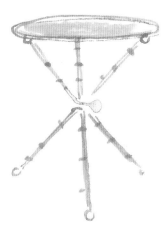

STYLE TIP
Balance the leggy excess in a room that comes from a lot of four-legged tables and chairs with some denser pieces like an old trunk or a squat ottoman, a skirted table, or a cube-shaped occasional table.

Tables Begetting Tables Pulling tables up to other tables gives a room dimension, hides the empty space under a table, and offers even more hospitable surfaces upon which to set your things. A win-win-win situation.

When placing a lamp
on an end table, make
sure the bottom of
the shade is below
eye level when you're
sitting down. (You
don't want to see the
workings of the lamp or
the bulbs.) Fifty-eight
inches is a good height
from the floor to the
top of a table lamps.
The taller the table, the
lower the lamp.

End Tables

The tables that flank your sofa can host drinks and snacks and laptops, but their real role is to hold lamps at a good height. Typically, these side tables are grounded by a lamp around which a constellation of smaller, less mobile items gravitates. They often include styled arrangements of framed pictures, bowls, boxes, and ornaments of your choosing.

If you go with unmatched end tables (or lamps, for that matter—and you know you can), consider keeping their heights about even. What constitutes an end table is limited really only by height—they're usually twenty-five to thirty inches tall—and your imagination. A chest of drawers? Okay. A round pedestal table? Sure. A tall stack of coffee-table books? Unusual, but why not?

Beware of Too Much Dreary Brown Furniture!

Walk into the home section of any department store, and you couldn't be blamed for thinking furniture is supposed to be made only out of brown wood. It isn't! Too many brown pieces in a room is the surest way to suck the life out of it. Ever seen a room and and wondered why it looked like a bland hotel lobby? Brown! Bossy decorator Sister Parish would allow no more than three brown pieces in any one room. Look at a picture of a room you love, and unless you are a devotee of a Zen aesthetic, you will find the furniture to be a mix of tones and materials.

Some not-brown materials and finishes:
- Painted wood
- Pickled or stained wood
- Lacquer
- Lucite
- Metal
- Glass
- Fabric

COZIFICATIONS

I have grown a little tired of over-careful
decorations. Somehow the feeling of homeyness
is lost when the decorator is too careful.

—ELSIE DE WOLFE

When I asked my mother-in-law, one of the coziest creatures I know, what the word "cozy" meant to her, she said, "A big fire blazing away, the smell of good food cooking on the stove, a hot drink in winter or a cool one in summer—and being in the care of a wonderful host." All those things are indeed super cozy, and I love them all, but this chapter is about decorating. What I call cozifications—those things that add dimension to a space, like rugs, textiles, throws, and pattern—are what we can incorporate into our rooms to achieve these same warm feelings. In fact, without decorative cozifications, a hot drink or a blazing fire wouldn't feel quite as welcoming.

For instance, picture yourself in a photo spread from a magazine like *Dwell*. You're sitting with a nice cup of tea on, say, an Eames chair that floats alone on an expanse of concrete floor in front of a fire burning in a square cut into the drywall. Interesting? Sure. Cozy? Not so much. Minimalism is single-dimension decorating. Cozifiers add layers.

Previous pages:
The sitting room of the former Deborah Mitford, Dowager Duchess of Devonshire, at Chatsworth is grand and completely cozy with its plain linen and faded chintz-covered seating, a furry rug, a tapestry-covered ottoman loaded with books, and lots of flowering plants.

Cozy decorating was perfected by the English in the postwar era. The ideal of faded chintzes, comfortable armchairs, lots of soft cushions, and flowers and books everywhere exudes the glorious imperfection that is the essence of English country-house style. Yet, like perfectly mussed hair, it is quite calculated. Its devil-may-care attitude of tossed cushions and seemingly haphazard pattern combinations is a bit of a lie, but one that in the telling becomes true. In other words, cozifications create a home that looks loved and lived-in, which in turn creates a home that *is* loved and lived-in.

Think of your chair
as host to a cushion.
The two work best
as counterpoints
in terms of color,
pattern, and texture.
Think silk on velvet,
needlepoint on
linen, faux leopard
on shiny chintz.

Throws Whether made of cashmere, soft wool, or cotton, throw blankets are a form of mobile decor that can travel from room to room slung over our shoulders. As long as they're meant to be used, even just draped over the arm of a sofa, they signal that a room is prepared to offer comfort. They're as ready for a solo catnap as they are to spread across children's laps, to create a little community of movie watchers. Throws manage to comfort us when we're feeling low, and warm us in a way that cranking up the heat can't.

When my daughter was about six, she wrote a little poem for my birthday. "Me and you, you and me", it went, "wrapped in a blanket, in front of the fire, the two of us as one." Interestingly, we had never sat together under a blanket in front of a fire. But the idea was as powerful as the real thing. Ever since then I've been sure to have throws around, ready to create actual memories.

When mixing patterns, the rule is to connect through color and contrast through scale. For instance, if you have two florals, they should share a color or two, but one should be a tiny pattern and one large or bold. Or if you have two stripes, make sure they have a hue in common, but let one be narrow stripes and one wide.

Textiles If throws warm people, textiles warm rooms. By "textile" I mean a decorative piece of woven fabric, like a quilt, blanket, or tapestry, that you can drape over a table, lay on a bed, or use to cover the back of a sofa. Patterned textiles are especially fantastic for people with color commitment issues, as you can just rotate them out easily if you tire of them. And for those who own solid-color sofas (which is most of us), draping something visually interesting over it helps break up an otherwise hulking mass.

The idea with textiles is simply to introduce a nice pattern, a crafty bit of handiwork, or a pretty floral. An antique textile adds a richness of texture, but so does a homespun patchwork quilt or an old cotton bedspread. The very fancy New York decorator Bunny Williams says she trawls the very not-fancy Pier 1 Imports for inexpensive Indian bedspreads (cotton only, no synthetics!) to toss over the backs of sofas.

History Lesson

In her first book, *The Decoration of Houses*, written with the architect Ogden Codman in the 1890s, Edith Wharton railed against her era's aesthetic gluttony, a congestion of dark woods, engorged upholstery, and countless ornaments. The influence of her more classic, pared-down approach, based on good proportions and clean lines, is still felt today. While we mix styles and periods freely, it is not quite the knickknack free-for-all it was for our Victorian forebears. More is definitely not more in the cozification department.

Insta-Cozy Couch

(1 blanket centered over back + 2 matching square cushions in corners + 1 rectangular cushion in center)

An easy way to
integrate cushions
into a room is to
obey the "law of
threes," in which you
repeat a color in the
cushions in at least
three things around
the room—like rugs,
curtains, walls,
or objects like a vase,
a throw, or a lamp.

Fluffy Cushions Recognize that throw cushions are not just decorative accents to be neatly arranged on your sofa. They are cozifiers, and as such, a soft one should be tossed onto nearly every upholstered chair, plus a few onto the sofa. The other day I was fussing about and put a big, squishy cushion on a chaise because I thought it looked good. That afternoon, a visiting friend curled up and took a blissful nap there. Only I knew that the nap was courtesy of the newly placed cushion. The humble cushion has outsize ability to set the tone of a room, both visually (pretty!) and physically (comfy and inviting!).

For a cushion resting against the back of an upholstered chair or sofa to be an invitation to sit down, the cushion needs to be soft, to give when you lean against it. This is the opposite of those hard, stiff, fussily arranged cusions that populate overly decorated rooms. You've seen them: bullet-like squares, stuffed to bursting, perched precariously on a diagonal or with their tops karate-chopped into submission. The message those cushions broadcast is "Please don't sit here, or at least don't mess me up!"

Not sure if your cushions are soft enough? If your family or friends ignore them or move them aside when they sit—or worse, toss them overboard when they want to cozy up—chances are they're too stiff or there are too many of them.

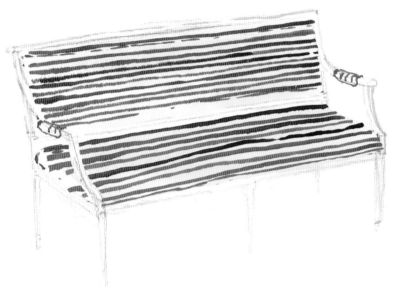

Ticking Stripes All stripes have a wonderfully sensible, relaxed quality about them. Because of their simplicity (straight, parallel lines), they are inherently unfussy, but none more so than mattress ticking. Mattress ticking is the thick cotton or linen fabric with narrow vertical stripes originally used to keep the straw inside of straw mattresses. You can't get any more practical or humble than that.

When Sister Parish first brought this undergarment of a fabric into decorating circulation in the 1940s, it was considered super daring. As a proper just-married lady on the Upper East Side, she had draperies in her first apartment fashioned from it as a cost-saving measure.

This countrified fabric still offers instant understated and unpretentious chic—especially when used to cut any fanciness or pretension in a room. You only need a little of its graphic dash to make magic. On the seat of a rather fancy painted French armchair covered in gray velvet, I've stuck a charming little blue and white ticking-striped cushion, which loosens that chair right up. In fact, ticking works especially well on painted furniture, like Louis XIV-style chairs and settees, and their Swedish counterparts in the Gustavian style, because they share a little of its rusticated nature.

Checks Another fabric that instantly introduces some humble charm into a scheme is the basic check. Perhaps because checks have been used in country houses in both England and America for the past couple hundred years, they seem to possess an air of ruddy-cheeked wholesomeness. Consider using them on dining chairs, either as seat cushions or as slipcovers, or do as many good decorators do and cover only the back side of upholstered chairs with this pattern. Just like stripes, checks work to "check" the standoffishness of more luxurious fabrics and finishes.

Florals Unlike stripes and checks, which read as flat, florals provide a visual break, acting like a window with a view to the outdoors. A floral fabric can be blowsy and even a little noisy, where stripes and checks are rather quiet. How easy it is to bring lush peonies, roses, hydrangeas, or even vines into a room! Try a loose floral slipcover on a beloved old armchair or just some throw cushions on a sofa (and don't be afraid of adding a ruffled edge in the same fabric—a little ruffle is a sweet thing). Florals look particularly wonderful amid actual greenery on a covered porch or on a terrace. Smaller-scaled flower patterns are great peeking out from things like a little surprise, like on the lining of curtains or on a piece of wallpaper used to line a drawer.

English Style The quintessential old-fashioned country-house decorating recipe is to use a floral, a check, and a stripe together in a scheme.

Log Baskets Even if you have no fireplace and no use for split wood, you still might like the rugged texture of a nice big woven basket in your living room (or front hall). In both the grandest houses and the most modern, a good basket cozies without cloying. A basket gives you something a little rough and real to break up the modern and sleek as much as the antique and refined. And who doesn't need an extra place to stash things? Newspapers, toys, or magazines in the living room. Boots or woolens in the hallway.

If you can stuff it with logs, all the better. And the bigger the better. With a log basket (with logs), always err on the too-big side, because then it will be just right.

A Bit of Ugly This might sound counterintuitive, but to create a beautiful home, you need a bit of ugly. I'm not suggesting you go wrangle up some hideous piece of furniture that's been lurking in the basement. Instead, consider highlighting your pretty colors with a dash of dullness, a dollop of dreary.

For instance, think about a room in which all the colors are pretty pastels like duck-egg blue and green and cream: the look can go rather dollhousey and saccharine. If you were to include a little gray, dull black, or faded green (i.e., olive drab), those very same lighter colors would actually look fresher and more dynamic. It would make them pop and would ground them in a more sophisticated palette. Similarly, while most people go overboard on brown furniture, a bit of dreary brown wood, or dull finishes, can be a sobering and stablilizing influence in a space, especially one that has any excess of glamour or girliness.

If ugly scares you, know that it comes wholly endorsed by decorator John Fowler of Colefax and Fowler, who created some of the prettiest rooms ever. "Often an ugly color is introduced," he says, describing the secret recipe to his work, "such as a faded black or drab, to give counterpoint to colors that are sweet and clean." By "drab" he means a faded, dark, or muddy hue—a cloudy gray or a dull green—to subtly add depth and substance to a room. A little ugly fights the stilted, too perfect, decorator-showhouse look—which is the enemy of all things cozy.

A DOTED-ON BEDROOM

We are happy horizontal.

—ILSE CRAWFORD

As welcoming as we want all our rooms to be, the bedroom should be even more so: a place focused on our comfort and pleasure in every detail. It is this room more than any other that allows us to take refuge from the world and return to ourselves. It is our most private space, and it should be arranged to take care of us, rather than just be a crash pad or an overprogrammed home office/exercise room/storage dump.

Having what you love around you is important, but forcing this room to work double time diminishes its ability to offer you the sense of peace it ought to. It can be nice to bring a laptop into bed or do some work at a desk, but don't set up your whole office here. Roll out a mat for yoga, maybe, but don't park an Exercycle.

This is the room in which to indulge yourself. I don't believe in skimping on the bed or its linens, quilts, and pillows. A beautifully made bed can make us happy.

Previous pages:
The bedroom of the late Brooke Astor, designed by Albert Hadley, has a spring-like green and white palette, a spot for reading and writing, and some bold Alan Campbell fabrics on the bench and armchair.

How High: Thirty inches from the floor to the top of the mattress feels wonderfully high.
Straight On: Do not angle your bed into a corner or float it in the middle of the room. It's a bed, not a boat.
Airy Sides: Ideally, beds have ample room on either side. Climbing over someone to get into bed should not be a style choice.
Facing Where: The feng shui–ers say the bed should not face the door, but if your bed is the prettiest thing in the room, why not see it when you walk in? If you've got a great view or a fireplace instead, then by all means, take their advice.

A Big Bed Ahhh, the bed! How I love the bed! The bed is our great ally. It receives us when we are sad and when we are satisfied; when we need to empty our minds or have a big, fat think; when we want to be alone or fall into a happy pile with those we love. It is the central focus around which the room revolves, both decoratively and emotionally, and it is worthy of our lavish doting.

In the case of a bed (but very little else having to do with a house!), bigger is definitely better. Since the bed is the point of this room, it should offer you the luxury of spreading out on a Sunday morning with coffee and the newspaper or bringing in the whole family for a movie night. It's a bit stingy to squeeze two adults into a full-size bed; a kingsize, or even a super king, is definitely better, especially for fitting a brood. (The California king, which is longer and narrower, is a more elegant alternative.)

In addition to big, high is nice. Climbing into a bed simply feels better—and is certainly more ceremonious—than dropping down onto one. A high bed also allows you to take advantage of any views out the window you might have. According to the very proper English decorating firm Colefax and Fowler, the ideal level is high enough that when you're propped against your pillows, you can chat at eye level with a guest in a nearby chair! While most of us don't regularly receive guests from bed, the point is a good one.

Wake to Pretty Make sure the first thing you see when you pry open your eyes is something pleasing, like a piece of art or a nice mirror, rather than a straight shot into the closet or the bathroom.

An Upholstered Headboard For the bed frame, a four-poster draped with fabric is certainly the most dramatic and enveloping, and the favorite of decorators. But without the steady hand and practiced eye of a professional, a canopied bed is also the most complicated to pull off. Upholstered headboards, on the other hand, also elevate the bed from mere sleeping spot to luxurious event and don't require an expert. Fabric-covered headboards look tailored and refined, and are super comfy for leaning against while reading in bed.

You can find pretty good headboards in furniture stores, but you can also have one made to your own specifications by an upholsterer. If you can draw it, download it, or rip it out of a magazine, you can have it. An upholsterer can build the whole bed frame for you, and although the cost for customization will be greater, so will the quality. You'll be able to choose not only any design but also the height of the bed, and if you want, you'll be able to integrate the headboard fabric into a matching upholstered box-spring cover or bed skirt. While I like to maintain a healthy distance from a staple gun, you can also bypass the upholsterer entirely, find a how-to video online, and do it your *own* self.

A Cocooned Room

Whether do it yourself or do it somebody else, going custom means you can also match the headboard fabric to your curtains or chair fabric if you so desire. The French pioneered this idea with scenic toiles de Jouy in the nineteenth century, covering walls, windows, and more in the same fabric. Particularly in a guest bedroom, all this matching fabric can feel pleasingly cocoon-like.

Cotton: The best cotton sheets are woven in Italy from Egyptian cotton. I'd look for this before fretting over thread count, which if too high is heavy and oppressive anyway.
• *Percale* is matte and crisper looking, and also cooler in summer.
• *Sateen* is shiny, and because it is thicker, warmer in winter.
Linen: Linen sheets are the thickest, and yet the most deliciously cool, making them ideal for summer. Plus, they improve with age and washing—getting even softer and more wonderful—and so can be passed down over generations.

Excellent Bed Linens I don't know why we tend to skimp on our own pleasure—perhaps it's our puritanical past—but I can't say enough about buying the best bed linens you can afford. This is a luxury you will indulge in every single day! Nothing beats sliding into bed between cool, crisp linens.

Everything that touches your skin should feel wonderfully soft and be natural. You've got to be a snob when it comes to sheets: no poly, no synthetics, no blends—no way! They feel scratchy, don't breathe, and don't last. When you're plunking down more than you think you ought to for your bed linens, remember, the better the quality, the longer they'll endure.

It is a great luxury and a huge treat to sleep on freshly ironed sheets. Should you not have your own in-house laundress, treat yourself to getting them professionally laundered and pressed. (Once you've been to the other side, it's hard to go back.) If you try this at home, know that cotton sateen needs less ironing than percale, and that linen sheets are the most difficult to iron. But there are new "vintage" linens that are meant to have a cozy, rumpled look, so that you won't need or want to iron them at all.

Better with Age You can find excellent vintage linens, especially in countries like Argentina, France, Portugal, Italy, and Spain, which have a tradition of embroidered linens.

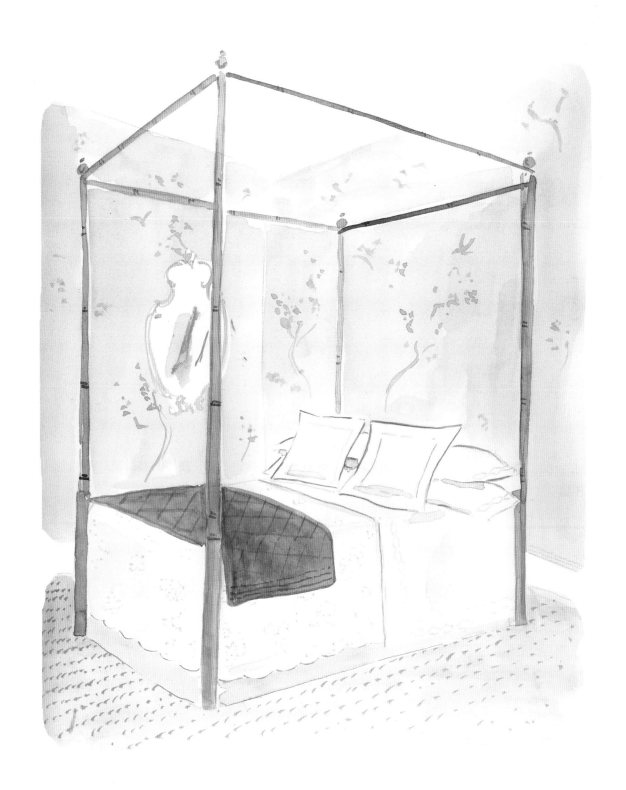

Quilts and Coverlets My ideal top layer is a pretty sheet folded over a beautiful patterned coverlet or a soft, solid quilt. In summer I also love a loose white matelassé and in winter a thick wool blanket tucked in tightly. I think the simplicity and ease of a soft, plump white duvet pulled all the way up looks sexy in other people's homes, but in mine it always reminds me of the lumpy surface of the moon.

A throw folded at the foot of the bed brings in a nice pattern, color, or texture to complement the main cover. But more important, throw blankets are perfect for pulling up around you for a midday nap. For this you want something super soft, like cashmere, or an old, worn-in quilt.

Experiment a little with your bedding, trying out different textures and styles. Contrast perks up a bed: Mix some thick linen pillow covers with shiny sateen sheets, or some super feminine flowery covers with a rough wool blanket or a handmade Indian quilt.

Not Too Many Pillows There are two kinds of pillows: the ones we use and the ones that end up on the floor. One or two, or maybe three, decorative pillows can work, but after that your bed starts to look like the Bloomingdale's floor model and requires its own staff to manage every evening before bed.

I understand the instinct to break up the big, boring landscape of the bed's surface with color and pattern. Both squares, those wonderfully large pillows, and a throw pillow or two can do the trick, though. You can find washable covers for square pillows in loads of wonderful patterns and designs; these will seem more like gorgeous textiles than plain cotton pillowcases do, and so they'll add a layer of polish and finish to a bed.

Pillow Recipe (serves two)

4	1 or 2	1
down-filled standards	**smaller pillows**	**Square**
Thirty-inch for queen or larger for king, for actual sleeping. If you have allergies, go for natural, non-animal materials.	Either a boudoir pillow—those dainty tiny things—or a small throw pillow for resting an elbow or your neck while reading or watching TV.	A twenty-six-inch square pillow that is great for propping yourself up on to read. Make sure it is firm, not limp and squishy.

There are many ways
to prop your pillows.
Square Finish: Stack
a pair of standard
pillows, and lean
a square pillow in front
of them.
Domino Effect: Lean
the large square pillow
upright against the
headboard with the
other pillows leaning
up against it in
descending size order.
Standard Issue: Skip
the square pillow,
and just stack the
standards and add
a few little pillows
resting against them
for a bit of a flourish.

Making the Bed (fancy)

1) **Bottom Sheet:** Using a gener-
ously sized flat sheet for the base
(flat sheets lie better and tuck more
neatly than fitted ones), lay it evenly
over the bed, and smoothly tuck
it in at the bottom and top edges.
Then make "hospital corners."
(Lift a corner triangle of sheet fabric
up onto the bed and tuck in the
part that remains below, then lower
the triangle and tuck it in.) Then
tuck in the sides.

2) **Top Sheet:** Lay a second flat
sheet over the bed with its top side
facing the mattress so that it will
be visible when the sheet is folded
back. Pull the sheet up so it is even
with the top of the bed. Make sure
the sides have an even amount
of sheet hanging over them. Tuck in
the bottom end.

3) **Blankets:** Lay a blanket (thin in
summer, wool in winter) over the
bottom three-quarters of the bed.
Tuck in the bottom.

4) **Coverlet, Quilt, or Duvet:** Lay
a coverlet over the blanket, its
top edge meeting the top of the
blanket. Fold the sheet down over
both. You can either let the sides
drape sweetly over the sides of
the bed or tuck them in for a more
buttoned-up look.

5) **Pillows:** Fluff your pillows and set
them on the bed, either laying flat in
a stack like pancakes or up against
the headboard, like dominoes.

6) **Extra Blanket:** Add a soft throw
at the base of the bed, folded in
thirds, with the bottom edge of the
blanket flush with the bottom edge
of the bed. Voilà!

Making the Bed (fast)

1) Tuck in the bottom sheet.

2) Lay the top sheet over it,
fold it over, and tuck it in.

3) Pull a duvet up to the top of
the bed.

4) Put pillows on top.

5) Go.

A Bottom-of-the-Bed Perch To complete the cocoon, the empty spot at the foot of your bed is the perfect place for a small piece of furniture to sit on. This is particularly true if your bed faces the door, as it is nice to see something pretty at the boring end of the bed when you walk in. An upright love seat, a single long bench, or a pair of small benches all make excellent punctuations, places to perch or fling your clothes onto.

Outfitting Guest Quarters

No one expects Four Seasons service, but too often spare rooms are repositories for unwanted furniture, cracked soaps, and swiped hotel toiletries. Think fresh, clean, and simple. Junky furniture can benefit from a rejuvenating coat of white or black paint to harmonize disparate pieces and hide all manner of flaws.

Essential
- Freshly laundered linens
- A full set of pillows
- An extra blanket
- A new bar of soap

Very Nice Indeed
- An empty closet with hangers
- Drawers free of your out-of-season clothes
- A wastebasket
- Some good books (short stories and essays are best)

The Extra Mile
- A scented candle
- Writing paper and pens
- A bunch of flowers
- A carafe of water
- Good bath oils

Before Guests Arrive
Throw open the window while you do a last-minute fluff. And every so often, do an overnight test-drive to see that things are in order.

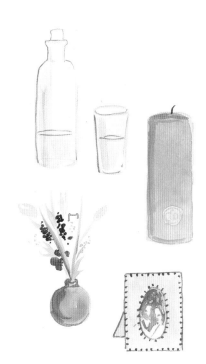

The Bedside Table One of my very favorite bedside tables is a simple fabric-covered round table. I know that might seem very Mario Buatta circa 1985, but if you don't use chintz and don't stick a piece of round glass on top of it, it won't veer in that direction.

A skirted table is a wonderful way to bring a beautiful floral or a pretty pattern into a room. It affords a great big surface and instant style. Because the fabric grazes the floor, the table itself can be a cheap folding thing from Ikea or any wrecked old round table you happen to have around. (And if you must, although I'd rather you didn't, you can stash things under the skirt.)

Alternatively, you can use a rectangular table or an actual desk for a bedside table, which allows you to pull up a chair and use it as a writing surface or a dressing table. (Having a desk in your bedroom does not violate my no-office-in-the-bedroom mandate.)

There are really no rules—a night table could be a set of drawers, a low set of open shelves, or even a square sofa side table. If you only have a small night table, you may need or want another to handle overflow. This trick of tables looking as if they are begetting smaller tables is very stylish: layered, practical, and chic. For instance, if your table surface can't contain your large pile of books or stacks of magazines, a little occasional table may be just the thing. This can be a footstool, a bench, or even a chair. When I need to call in reinforcements, I pull in a low African stool from the living room and park it in front of the bedside table.

NICE TO KNOW

• A table at the same level or a little higher than the bed looks best and is the most comfortable.
• Bedside tables need not match—or be topped by identical lamps, for that matter.
• If you go for unmatched tables and unmatched lamps, keep their overall height uniform.

PRETTY
NECCESSITIES
• Scented candles
• Flowers
• Framed photos
• Books
• Pad and pencils

A Bedside Command Center If the bed is your relaxation HQ, the bedside table should work a bit like a control station operable from a supine position. The idea is to have at your disposal all those things you might like or need. It is nowhere more essential than by your bed that the pragmatic and the beautiful operate in concert. If it makes you happy to wake up to the sight of flowers, then a little bouquet is entirely functional. But while an array of remotes splayed out beside you might be practical, it is usually unfortunate to behold. It is often a challenge to resolve the two. The stuff we have bedside falls either into the category of pretty necessities or into that of necessities that need to be prettified.

Definitely include a couple of things that just bring joy and look nice, like framed pictures. Try putting a vase of flowers next to your bed–even when you're not having people over–and see how good it makes you feel.

It is a sign of a together person to have a pad of paper and a cup of pens or pencils at the ready when that brilliant idea strikes in the middle of the night (or when you bolt up in a panic remembering someone you forgot to call back two years ago). I have noticed that fancy people never search madly for something to write on or a working pen. They have placed a pretty pad (usually with their name or house address printed on it) and a container of pens and pencils (often identical, with sharp points facing up) in every place–from entry hall to kitchen–where they might be needed. (Nice, inexpensive custom notepads and pencils in every possible color are easy to find online.)

And as reading in bed is one of life's great pleasures, there should always be room by your bed for books. As old-fashioned as they may seem, books are comforting to have around, especially now that they are just one of several formats for reading.

NECESSITIES, PRETTIFIED

Use cups and baskets to contain these, trays to arrange them on, and boxes to hide them in.

- Remotes
- Hand cream
- Eyeglasses
- Post-its
- Paper clips
- Eye mask
- Tissues
- Jewelry
- Drinks glasses

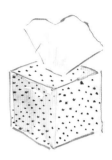

Tissues, Remotes, and Other Useful Things

While in photo shoots it often looks as if people survive with only a few perfectly chosen books, a striking objet, and a little pot of flowers at their bedside, real life requires things like eyeglasses, Post-its, hand cream, and tissues within easy reach. With these, your choice is basically either to stow them or show them. I tend to like an honest display of useful items—like TVs and jewelry and towels—and yet in the bedroom I mostly go for discreet concealment.

If hiding things away seems too fussy, a small tray can make any and all random bits look pulled together. The great American decorator Albert Hadley has practically made an art installation out of his bedside necessities, arranging them with such flair that a television remote, a lighter, some notebooks, and a bunch of pens have the stark intentionality of a Mondrian (see illustration at left). If you spend a little time arranging your belongings (think of them as shapes and try to make a composition), and especially if you add in some pretties like books or flowers, you can reform even the worst criminals of style, like hideous tissue boxes, aggressively techy-looking cordless phones, and the myriad remotes required to operate a single TV.

While remotes can quite nicely be collected upright in an open basket or lined up on a tray, I can't bear to have them near me, and they are stashed in a box across the room. And while it may seem dorky to hide tissues in those slipcover thingies, it is not as dorky as it is outrageous that no one has yet managed to design an acceptable-looking box of tissues. And by the time someone makes a decent-looking phone, landlines probably won't even exist. Banishing the cordless to my husband's side of the bed hasn't completely solved the problem, but I do look at my bedside more than his. I've noticed that the über stylish often set a little telephone table in front of their night table (see page 117) and put pens and paper on it as well. This keeps the hardworking things a bit lower down and leaves the bedside table free for the pretties.

BATH AS
A ROOM

A bathroom can and should be
an exciting room to go into.

—DAVID HICKS

For a room so vital to our lives, why is the bathroom so often a decorating afterthought? Much consideration is given to the fixtures and
hardware (I'll give none to those here), and yet relatively little to the
decorative pleasures this room can provide (and on which I will happily
expound). Bathing is as much about recharging and blissfully doing nothing as it
is about cleansing. The setting should offer charm and delight, not simply efficient
plumbing and clean surfaces.

The iconoclastic twentieth-century decorator Elsie de Wolfe was the first
to create a modern bathroom that rose above pure business. The idea of
a bathroom where one might actually wish to linger was quite revolutionary,
and decoration made her revolution possible. Her "bath salon" decadently
boasted mirrored columns and a mirrored fireplace, a zebra-covered chaise,
taps shaped like swans' heads, and hooks in the form of dolphins. While that
might be excessive, she also covered the walls in beautiful wallpaper and hung
framed art—quite reasonable ideas.

The lesson of subverting this room's typical chrome and tile hegemony is
one worth heeding. Your lav need not shine like some hygienic lab. While
bathrooms share many of the same elements as the rooms in the rest of our
homes—like mirrors, lighting, and storage—we tend to
decorate them with fixtures we buy at specialty stores.
Bust out of this box a bit, hit your favorite shops, and
include some actual furniture (like the kind you stick in
other rooms), maybe even a patinated old piece or two.
As in any other room, you want to warm up the space,
and imbue it with the feeling of well-lived life.

Previous pages: This
bathroom designed
by Muriel Brandolini
has the charm of
a real room thanks
to wallpaper, pictures,
a chandelier, and
some greenery.

Chairs and Stools The opportunity to have a nice chair in the bathroom is too often overlooked. If you've got space, there are few things more welcoming and homey than a comfy seat near the tub, whether for a child to come and chat while you soak or just as an alternative to the floor as a place to toss your clothes. Any kind of chair is nice, but if it's upholstered it should be covered in some durable (washable) cotton or terry cloth.

As an alternative (if you don't have a lot of space), or in addition (if you do), a big chair, a little bench, or a stool can work well to promote the spirit of the bath as a room. You can also perch a book and a cup of tea here while you soak, or use it to stack a neat pile of towels. That somehow always looks to me like an invitation to have a nice shower or bath, in a way that towels hanging on a bar never do.

Some Bathside Perches
• Slipper chair
• Armchair
• Chaise
• Garden or bistro chair
• Footstool
• Bar stool
• Ceramic garden drum

Mirrors and Lamps Ditching the standard-issue medicine cabinet for a nice, antique mirror made for one of the most dramatic, quick changes any room of mine has ever undergone. That simple switch instantly brought warmth and beauty to the cold, hard surfaces of the bathroom. There is simply no reason (other than storage) that the mirror/cabinet must look as if it hails from an apothecary, if that is not your style. (And if you buy a light-weight mirror, you can have it hinged so you can still use the "guts" of the cabinet. Storage problem solved.)

Likewise, who decreed that the lights over the mirror must look like they were swiped from a schoolhouse during the Great Depression? Obviously those lights have to make sure every blemish or whisker is clearly accounted for and addressed, but there are many kinds of sconces or fabric-shaded lights that can work as well as more typical bathroom light fixtures.

Of course we now know that a chandelier dangling from the middle of the room is perfectly acceptable. But wall lamps should also be integrated into the bathroom repertoire. I am a huge fan of all that a little lamp can do (see the Nice Lighting chapter) to add personality, style, and a warm glow to a room—and which room needs those things more than this one?

Tables and Vanities This brings me to the surfaces upon which we might place a lamp. If you've got room, you can use a dressing table. This needn't be an overly girly Jean Harlow fantasy setup (although it can be). But the more this room acts like a boudoir, transitioning you kindly into the day, the better. And if you've got a place to sit, that is certainly nicer than leaning over the sink and having makeup drop all over the place.

I am partial to painted wood in a bathroom, and to the subtle femininity of a cabriole leg. But any small table, even if there is no room for pulling up a little perch to it, is perfect for a plant, some hand towels, or a tray of perfumes or bath oils.

More Bins, Bowls, and Baskets

As for the smalls of a bathroom, the same principle holds: no one is forcing us to shop at Bed Bath and Beyond for matching trash cans, soap dishes, and toothbrush cups. Why squander so many decorative opportunities?

A first stop for sprucing up the sink-side necessities for drinking, toothbrush corralling, and soap setting could well be your own pantry. Is there an unusual-looking glass, a nice mug for toothpaste, a pretty saucer for rings or soap, or a less-than-perfect silver tray that could hold your fragrances?

Slightly further afield, vintage shops and garage sales are treasure troves for bath odds and ends like big antique hooks for the back of door and the ever useful baskets or wire bins.

As someone who believes that supplies should be abundant and easy to find, I prefer an ample grouping of toilet paper piled up in an old washbowl or tote rather than a single roll dangling its wispy offering from a hospital-like rod on the wall. And why use a plastic bin for the garbage when a basket would do? I especially adore baskets or wire bins in cabinet shelves for parsing the meds from the makeup, and mine from his.

Bathroom Basket Mania

There is a basket in every shape and size (from small cylinders to giant hampers) for every bit and bob that needs wrangling, such as:

- cotton balls and swabs
- combs or makeup brushes
- trash
- towels
- toilet paper
- toiletries

NICE TO KNOW

These items can just as easily come from your cupboard as they can from a bath shop:
- Drinking glass
- Vessel for toothbrushes
- Dish for soap
- Bowl for jewelry
- Cups for lipstick and makeup brushes
- Tray for toiletries

Folding a Towel
The goal is nice flat
squares that all look
the same, are easy
to store, and look
super satisfying in
a neat stack.
1) Lay the towel out on
a flat surface and fold
it in half lengthwise.
2) Then fold it in half
once more from the
short end.
3) Fold the short end
in half one more time.
Voilà!

Decent Bath Linens In other areas of decor, an honest, lived-in look
is cool and appealing, but this is not the case with your towel wardrobe.
Bath linens are not the place to seek out patina. Yet too often towels are
fraying, bath mats are nasty, and shower curtains are barely considered.
Take stock every so often to see if you need an upgrade: towels should be
large, absorbent, and in good condition; your bath mat should not have
passed its sell-by date; and the shower curtain should be *complètement
sans* grunge. In summer, Turkish hammam towels made from thin cotton
are super lightweight, surprisingly absorbent, and quick drying. They look
wonderful wrapped around your waist at the beach or just hanging from
a hook in the bathroom.

STYLE TIP
Friends, bath mats
are not area rugs!
To keep them fluffy
and clean, they
should be lifted
from the floor and
hung over the
tub between uses.

Nice Shower Curtains

One strike against plastic shower curtains is evident as soon as you unwrap one—that odor of a science experiment gone wrong. A good shower curtain is something that can be tossed in the wash every so often along with your towels. Whether super simple (like a waffle-weave cotton or a glazed linen) or more decorative (like John Robshaw's graphic, patterned prints), shower curtains take up a lot of real estate and thus ought to be attractive.

Pictures on the Wall

Not only are pictures hanging on the wall great for room-ing up your bathroom, but bathrooms are also ideal places for framed photographs that may be a little too personal for more public spaces. Snapshots of private moments on holiday, pics of flowers from the garden, or images with (or by) children are nice for us, and for guests to chance upon. You can be more laissez-faire here than in public rooms, and even cover the walls with snapshots or postcards dorm room-style. No one is really judging. The key is to invite your personality in, as you would in a regular room.

GLAMIFICATIONS

> Use your mirrors . . . and you will
> multiply the pleasures of your room.
>
> —ELSIE DE WOLFE

Given how many mundane tasks a house must perform, a bit of frippery is actually a necessity. It can elevate a room into an experience. Glamour does require guts, though, because you need to express it with a bold stroke, not a tentative gesture. What creates glamour? Sparkle! Shine! Embellishment! Color! Pattern! Glamour is an essential excess, the icing on our cake.

Don't think I am suggesting that we all have to go for an over-the-top, glitzy Hollywood "more is more" kind of look. In fact, that is rather hard to pull off. Miles Redd, a decorator who does not fear the glam, pulls out all the stops—crystal chandelier, gilded wood, chinoiserie wallpaper, leopard fabric, etc.—but keeps a tight rein on the color palette. You can also be selective and elegant, choosing perhaps one brilliantly ornate mirror, a lavish wallpaper, or a single glittering chandelier, in an otherwise modern or refined room. You don't need to overdo it, but you can't be wimpy: that chandelier or that mirror or wallpaper has to assert itself loudly and clearly. Glamour is not meek.

Simplicity and glamour, hand in hand, make for a fresh and chic combination. Case in point: Yves Saint Laurent's living room in Tangiers. Unlike the designer's usual über-maximalist style, this room is super restrained. A pretty floral chintz is set off by white walls adorned only with a few rustic plates, allowing a large and gorgeous gold mirror by the artist Claude Lalanne and an exquisite Venetian glass chandelier to perform as the stars of the room. One can pick and choose, or tick off every glamour box, depending on one's inclination.

Previous pages: In his villa in Tangiers, Yves Saint Laurent worked with Jacques Grange to combine flowery chintz in airy settings with plenty of white space.

Wallpaper

It's hard to imagine that several years ago the only thing most people did with wallpaper was remove it. All of its potential to add pattern, style, color, excitement, and impact was dismissed. And for what? The hegemony of the boring white gallery-style wall! Dullsville.

Wallpaper can make a nothing space feel important. Particularly with small rooms, it can transform them into really special places. Small rooms often handle large-scale or busy patterns better than large rooms, where the pattern can be too much to take.

Rare is the room that can't benefit from some wallpaper. I love it even in bathrooms, where it adds nice texture and interest. (So long as the room has good ventilation.) Maybe kitchens are the only place in which the dominance of painted walls should remain unchallenged. Although I have seen great wallpapered backsplashes covered with glass. And really, what's a rule if not something meant to be broken?

Put It Here: Wallpaper

Save the super-crazy or big-patterned wallpapers for areas that are more passed-through than lived-in. A really bold motif in a living room can start to drive you crazy—and get boring—fast. Good spaces for mega-watt prints:

- Hallway
- Powder room
- Corridors
- Guest bedroom
- Guest bath
- Closet interiors

Lacquered Walls The most elegant-looking painted walls are shiny painted walls. They are smooth and shimmery; they reflect light and add a bit of intrigue. Somewhere along the decorative timeline, everyone seemed to decide collectively that a dull matte finish was best for their walls. This is not a self-evident, universal truth. True lacquered walls (requiring loads of coats and loads of dough) are, pardon the pun, brilliant. But a high-gloss enamel paint can do the trick too. Billy Baldwin once licked a gardenia leaf until it glistened like lacquer to show the painter the color he wanted.

Think about a shiny deep-red study or a shimmering loden-green hallway; but no matter what, think about a shiny room somewhere in your home calling out to you with its sophisticated, mysterious allure.

Decorative Mirrors If you only have mirrors for checking your face or your outfits, you don't have enough mirrors in your life. Most rooms can benefit from a mirror, as most lives can benefit from the extra sparkle.

Glamorous mirrors, as opposed to practical ones, have beautiful frames (like gold starbursts or red lacquer or designs carved from wood) and maybe even dark, smoky glass inside (either antique or antiqued) and are often hung in places where you can't even see yourself in them anyway (like above a fireplace). Convex mirrors (those round, protruding ones) have been used since classical times to reflect light, not to check your eyeliner. This is still the point of the glamorous mirror, convex or otherwise. That and just being a big beautiful object that can create the kind of drama that grounds a room.

For a couple of years I stewed over a gigantic painting belonging to my husband that hung above the fireplace. I fantasized about how glorious our space could be if only I had a big gilt mirror in that very spot. When I finally won the battle and the painting was retired to our bedroom, the resulting transformation wildly exceeded my hopes. The big mirror—heavy yet delicate, commanding yet airy—gave the room focus while bringing an ethereal cool to the entire space, and was a gorgeous counterpoint of grandeur in what is essentially a modern room. The old mirror tosses the daylight around and multiplies the light of the chandelier reflected in it, and the glimmer of lit candles on the mantel in front of it. A highly functional decorative object if ever there was one.

THIS IS HOW

Reflecting Light
If you want to throw some light into a dark room, place a mirror on the wall perpendicular to the window, not across from the window as is commonly done, and which actually bounces the light right back out the window!

Put It Here: Mirrored Panels

While these can seem very 1970s Miami Grandma, the light-enhancing powers of mirrored panels are not to be overlooked. Try them:

- behind shelves
- as a kitchen backsplash
- inset into cabinet fronts
- as trim on the front edge of bookshelves
- on the chimneypiece, from mantel to ceiling
- on cornices
- on the side and top panels of deeply set windows

Put It Here: Decorative Mirrors

Make sure that whatever is directly across from the mirror is something lovely. It could be a window with a nice view outside, in which case you're choosing to bring that view into the room over having the window's light reflected into the room. Try them:

- above the fireplace
- in between a pair of tall windows
- above any console or dresser, in the bedroom, or hallway
- on the floor leaning against a wall
- above a sofa
- in a dining room

Tassels and Fringe Known by the lovely French word *passemen-terie,* decorating notions like ribbon and trim, tassels and fringe add embellishment to lampshades, curtains, and upholstery. Again, this can be an elaborate process—custom designed and handmade by craftsmen in France—or a simple one, with notions from a ribbon or craft store, glue-gunned or tacked to the fabric's edge.

Drippy Chandeliers Chandeliers have been addressed in the lighting chapter, but they also deserve a special shout-out here in the glam department. As my friend Rita says, the ones that twinkle and charm the most are those chandis that look like "some old dowager's jewelry." The more bits of crystal there are, the more refracting, dispersing, and reflecting you'll have going on.

The impact of one of these old-fashioned pieces where it really stands out—in a modern kitchen, a simple dining room, or a child's room, for example—is greater than in a fancy or traditional room. And amp things up further by making sure the chandelier's fluttering light is reflected in a mirror. Insta-magic!

Old-fashioned Writing Tables Fancy twentieth-century decorators couldn't get enough of the writing table as a signifier of a gracious home and a gracious host. Doyenne of decor Elsie de Wolfe thought the dining room and the bathroom were the only rooms where it wasn't essential to have one. The writing table in the Internet age is a modern-day frippery, because while a little useful, it is mostly pretty. It is not some hardworking office desk paired with an ergonomic wheely seat, but rather a delicate piece of furniture, maybe with a drawer, and an attractive, comfortable-enough chair to perch on while you compose a handwritten missive.

Why bother with a quaint relic of a time when people communicated principally by letters? This is why: because like lunch on the lawn or a candlelit dinner, sitting down at a proper little table is entirely gracious. It is about the necessity of charm. And having a nice table in the living room tucked in front of a window or behind the sofa gives the room an expanded sense of purpose.

Decorator Mark Hampton thought the writing desk was the most essential item in a guest bedroom. (After the bed, I suppose.) And as a houseguest, I find it really nice to have a private place of my own to sit and make some calls or answer e-mails. A writing desk is a detour stopping you from going directly into the bed or onto the sofa with a laptop.

The Table, Accessorized
The pretty table needs pretty things upon it:
• Writing paper
• Notepads
• A letter rack
• Pens and sharpened pencils in nice cups
• Stamps and paper clips in little bowls or boxes
• A decorative object or two whose intent is to charm
• Flowers (fragrant, ideally)
• A scented candle

A Little Animal Print
As effective as it is divisive, animal print, even its faux form, infuses a sense of raciness and exoticism—a whiff of the wild—into our highly domesticated arrangements. I wouldn't advise more than a single dose per room; a little animal goes a long way.

I prefer the small-scale patterns, like cheetah and leopard print, which look great on small pieces like throw pillows or a little upholstered chair or footstool. But even wall-to-wall, a leopard-print carpet in a bedroom or a library can also be crazy chic. When used over a larger expanse like this, the pattern becomes a quiet, almost neutral background.

The larger-scaled patterns like zebra and pony might be reaching their saturation point, though, and need to be given a little time off to avoid cliché. Whereas cheetah and friends have been the domain of stuffy Upper East Siders for so long, they're due for a downtown, hipster embrace.

Shiny Objects
Like magpies, we are attracted to bright, shiny objects, and for good reason: our homes need them. As our eyes flit around the room, they alight on and are delighted by those bright spots. Especially if your style veers toward the earthy, a bit of sparkle brings a focused sharpness to the look of natural materials and organic shapes.

These objects can be in silver, gold, brass, glass, or mirror, and in the form of anything from boxes to bowls to candlesticks to picture frames or even completely useless items like shapes or figurines whose only purpose is decorative.

Think of these things as bright points of punctuation breaking up the long run-on sentence that is your home. Set shiny things upon consoles, inside shelves, atop books. Mingle them, make tableaux of them, set them on a pedestal. Just don't overlook them.

DINNERS
WITH
FRIENDS

Decorating has to do with people and beauty
and the timeless activities of domestic life.

—MARK HAMPTON

Think about the difference between a meal with friends in a restaurant
and one at home. (Don't think about the difference in the amount of
work!) When friends are in our home, around our table, bonds form
and friendships deepen much more quickly.

Most of us don't entertain as often as we'd like, in part because we wish to offer
a level of style that's hard to eke out of our busy days. The simple solution of having
whatever you need on hand means that you're less likely to
be scurrying around in a frenzy rifling through cupboards
when friends arrive, and more likely to be kicking back with
them. The first duty of a host is to be of good cheer—without
that, the rest can get tossed out the window for all it will
matter. Herewith a few preemptive measures, basic pieces,
and useful tips for keeping house and laying tables.

Previous pages:
An antique textile-
covered table, inspired
by the one in Janet
de Botton's house in
Provence. (Her table
is actually surrounded
by floor-to-ceiling
plates, not books.)

I don't do any of this,
but I wish I did.
• Keep glasses upside
down on shallow, felt-
covered shelves.
• Store trays vertically.
• Keep napkins folded
by color in drawers.
• Drape tablecloths
over pants hangers to
reduce wrinkles.

A Well-Stocked Pantry When I visit a beautifully run home (usually belonging to a fancy decorator or a rich person), I am as fascinated
by what's hidden away as by what's on display. A little snooping almost
always reveals an orderly pantry with entertaining supplies lined up like
patient soldiers waiting to serve. It's not just the sheer volume of linens
and vases and platters and the ready supplies of candles, tea lights, and
votives that impress. Although they do. It's how beautifully they're organized. Here are a couple of secrets I've stolen: use a label maker to ID
the front of each shelf with what goes where. (This is to keep the staff
from mixing things up, but it works equally well when you are your staff.)
And toss the broken, ripped, stained, and chipped, plus those things you
never use but think you will someday. They are making it hard to find
what you need, and therefore planning is that much more difficult.

If you take the time to arrange items neatly, press linens before you
need them, and order supplies like candles in bulk, you will be rewarded
with a wave of domestic satisfaction every time you see them.

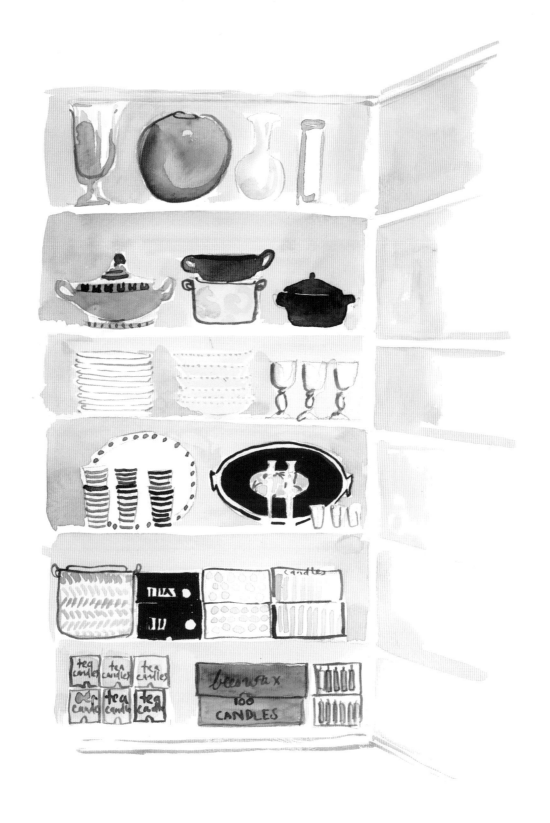

A Drinks Table Having a permanent drinks station as part of your decor is welcoming and cozy and very, very useful. Think about that often awkward moment when guests first arrive and are just standing around. A drinks table allows them to help themselves or fix someone else a drink. Being useful makes people feel at home. Plus, bar setups look so pretty—all those bottles and glasses and bits of silver.

You can arrange one on any surface: its very own table, a console sharing space with books and lamps, or even a tall shelf in a bookcase.

Go the extra style mile with a tray upon which to organize your bottles and glasses, colorful cocktail napkins, a pretty bowl for nuts, a candle or a little lamp, and maybe a small bouquet.

Bar Accessories
Aside from alcohol, sodas, and mixers, you might want:
- a tray for bottles
- a bottle opener
- an ice bucket (a cylindrical glass vase works)
- tongs or a big spoon
- a shaker
- glasses (tall, short, and stemmed)
- cocktail napkins
- a little cutting board and knife for lemons and limes

Coffee and Tea Service

Who can resist having a warm drink and something delicious delivered to them on a tray—whether in bed, by the fire, or in the kitchen? Children especially adore this kind of attention, and a tray with lemonade or hot cider and little treats scores you bonus points with them.

If you're lucky enough to have a nice coffee or tea set, don't let it gather dust on your shelf. If you don't have one, just round up a tray, one pot for coffee and one for tea, and a matching creamer and sugar bowl. The whole thing needn't match or even be all ceramic or all silver—in fact, it's even better if it's not.

Keep all the fixings together on a pantry shelf for effortless access. For me this stash includes loose teas and La Perruche sugar cubes (in brown and white, as they look good mixed), a pot of honey, and a supply of cookies like those delicious Petit Écolier ones from Lu that they have at the grocery store. Next time a friend drops by, you're set.

Covering a Round Table

Big round tables are notoriously difficult to find tablecloths for, but king-size coverlets (and even thick linen sheets) often fit perfectly! You can also have a base cloth that hits the floor custom made. (To measure for it, add the diameter of the table to two times its height.) Your dry cleaner can probably make it for you. You can then throw any tablecloth over it, changing that out or washing it as often as you like.

A Dining Table Don't despair if you don't yet have the table of your dreams. Dining room tables can be enormously expensive. Even many fancy style hounds, for whom money is no object, choose to simply cover a basic plywood table with floor-length fabric and then top it with a square tablecloth that can be changed out (and washed). This is insta-chic and super cheap!

No dining table at all? No excuse! A friend of mine has some of the liveliest and prettiest dinner parties I've ever been to, and yet her apartment is so small there's not even a place to eat breakfast. Instead, some people sit around the coffee table, some perch on the sofa, plates on laps, and others sit on the rug. It's amazing how social stiffness flies right out the window when someone's butt is on the ground.

One needn't take a meal around a coffee table or in the living room out of necessity. It's fun to eat in unusual spots around the house, like in the front hall or in a study—or even in that rarely used room: the dining room.

What Shape Table?

Round: Round tables are probably the most convivial, as they allow not only chats between people seated next to each other but a single conversation among the group as well.

Long: Long tables encourage exchanges with those directly across the table as well as more intimate chats with those on one's right or left.

Square: To my eye, a square table looks great because it allows table-setting symmetry— a central bouquet flanked by four candlesticks—but if it fits more than four people, there can be a lot of dead space at the center, which doesn't encourage reaching across the wide chasm for a chat.

Deciding on a mood you want your table to convey will seriously cut down on stressful pre-party table fussing. Give yourself a verbal cue, like "spring garden" or "winter cabin" or "jewel tones," in order to keep all your table-setting elements blending harmoniously.

Pretty Table Settings

A beautiful table can make everyone around it feel sparkly and special, lifting spirits and enlivening the conversation. Setting a table is basic domestic ritual, and doing it for a party mixes creativity and a lovely sense of anticipation into the process. The decorator Charlotte Moss refers to table setting as "everyday decorating." Whatever you do, please don't reserve your best stuff for special occasions. Good things become more beloved the more they're used. Your finest and fanciest pieces can be dressed down with simple linens or plain glasses to get them into regular circulation. Dragging your indoor finery outside once in a while makes a backyard picnic feel incredibly festive.

Nonetheless, when in table-setting doubt, it is better to go underfancy than overfancy. If you pull out all your finest things at once, you'll probably make yourself—and your guests—feel uptight. A rumpled cloth, simple plates, and big cotton napkins can be just as gorgeous as your wedding china, a damask cloth, and cut crystal.

Diversifying Your Settings

Create multiple table-setting options by collecting extra pieces in one color scheme. Say you choose red; you can use just a dash—such as ruby-red drinking glasses mixed with your basics—or go whole hog with ruby-red drinking glasses, rosy platters, claret-colored napkins, and a crimson-edged tablecloth.

Wardrobe Essentials

This basic "wardrobe" of pieces allows you to whip up a table on a moment's notice:

- A serving tray
- Two platters
- Two serving bowls
- Two serving spoons and forks
- A wooden salad bowl and servers
- Dinner plates
- Dessert plates
- Glasses for wine and for water
- Cutlery
- A linen tablecloth
- Big white napkins (twenty-two inches)
- A pair of hurricane lanterns or candlesticks
- Votive holders
- A few small vases

STYLE TIP

A pressed tablecloth feels crisp and formal, but a rumpled one can feel relaxed and casual. For a rumpled, not wrinkled, tablecloth, line dry it or pull it from the dryer when it's still a little damp.

THIS IS HOW

Covering a Rectangular Table
Tablecloths need to come down at least several inches over the sides of the table. (As with a hemline, the farther it falls, the dressier it seems.) When in doubt, err on the side of too big: liberal proportions feel generous; small ones feel stingy.

A Stash of Table Linens A simple white tablecloth and some big white napkins are the little black dress of your table wardrobe. They go with anything, and if you add some candles flickering around your glasses and silver, you've got tabletop perfection. But little black dresses do not a wardrobe make. You'll also want colorful, printed table linens because they are jolly, and because they are the quickest and cheapest way to change the whole look of your table. It may be impossible to have too many tablecloths! I find that drab linens in grays and other earthy hues are as delightful as bright and cheery patterned ones. Oh, and vintage tablecloths! These finds can range from rough, peasanty linens made from old grain-sack fabric (you've seen them: plain linen with a few stripes either in red or blue) to very fine, delicately embroidered pieces. Who cares if the monogram isn't yours? In fact, who cares if a tablecloth is not a tablecloth at all? A linen sheet can dress a table perfectly well, as can a thin cotton bedspread or an inexpensive quilt. The only rule is, once again, no synthetics, please.

Candlesticks It's no great coincidence that the key to making people feel sparkly is to make the room itself sparkly. Candlelight, and low light in general, is essential for creating an elegant mood. The reason we still bother with candles, antiquated as they are, is that their light is hypnotic. And flattering. And it cannot be duplicated by any form of electric light. Candles mix best with dimly lit rooms. So keep all complementary lights low so that candlelight can cast its magic spell.

Get yourself at least one pair of real silver candlesticks. You will have them forever, and you can use them all the time. These classics go with anything and elevate everything. You don't need to rush out to Tiffany; old candlesticks are often more beautiful and less expensive than new, and can easily be found at flea markets and garage sales, and in your mother's cupboard.

Cheap Votives Keep on hand a stock of cheap glass votives and several packs of tea lights. When candlelight is below eye level it is the most flattering, plus votives give you the freedom to spread the sparkle wherever you want, not just on the table. I love them near plants and flowers, on a drinks tray, or on a bookshelf. Tea lights with clear plastic bottoms are, to my mind, an innovation that rivals the steam engine! No more wax sticking in the glass or tin-bottomed tea lights showing through the votives.

Hurricanes The hurricane is the fancier cousin of the votive. These are a secret weapon of decorators and for good reason: their shape is strong and sculptural, they provide a vertical focus to a table, and they can light up an area with more stylistic oomph than any skinny candlestick or short votive.

Put It Here: One or Two Hurricanes
- On a coffee table
- On the mantel
- On a sideboard
- On a console behind a sofa
- On a front hall table
- On the dining table (to keep it looking busy when it's not in use)

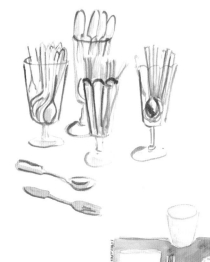

Old Silverware If you are lucky enough to have some good silver, use it! As with your fancy china, get this stuff out of the cupboard and onto the table. One of my favorite and most simple looks on a table is plain linen, rustic napkins, and good silver. Not being the beneficiary of any such inheritance, I've been amassing a little collection of unmatching vintage hotel utensils—silver-plated stuff that was used in hotels and restaurants—that does the trick and still feels substantial in your hand.

A PERSONAL
NARRATIVE

*Many people, as they accumulate things, just mix
them together any old way, assuming
that any sort of hodgepodge on a table will turn
out all right. They are dead wrong.*

—BILLY BALDWIN

O ur home tells a story about us, so we may as well take the opportunity to make it a stylish one. Our personal treasures—the art, photos, books, and decorative objects in our home—help define us. Those objects can form the clutter of one's house, or, through a bit of clever arrangement, they can be strung into a telling and pleasing narrative. Simply collecting is not enough; objects are like words that need to be made into meaningful sentences. Herewith, some styling tips.

Previous pages:
Illustrator Pierre
Le-Tan's love of art and
literature is apparent
at first glance in his
Paris apartment.

Books Books really do furnish a room. The less necessary they become as useful objects, the more important they become as decorative objects. We no longer need that dog-eared paperback from college to look up a quote from Hegel, and yet books are physical manifestations of our histories, our interests, and our passions. They are also beautiful creations of design and typography that evoke their era. There are plenty of anachronistic things that are essential for a comfortable home: we certainly don't need candlelight or blazing fires or antique mirrors but we love them for how they make us feel. Our books allow us to be surrounded by things we love and admire, and allow others to share in our interests without our even having to mention them.

Books make a room feel like a room. They are reassuring not just climbing up walls; rare is the horizontal surface that doesn't seem a little better off with a stack upon it. You can even pile books on the floor. There are many schools of thought on how to organize one's books—by color, size, subject, or author. To me, treating them just as color blocks takes the bookiness out of them, but to each his own. Regardless, shelves full of books definitely need to be broken up a bit with a few objects, pictures, and maybe some horizontal stacks.

Creating Diversity in Dense Walls of Books

Create cohesion with these recommended "smalls" by repeating certain colors, forms, or materials.

- Mix in some horizontal stacks of books among the vertical rows.
- Top a low pile of books with a small object—a vase or a little bowl.

- Intersperse objects, like candles, bowls, boxes, or sculptures, among the books.
- Interrupt rows of books with framed pictures.

- Hang framed pictures on the shelf fronts.
- Put a table (long and narrow or a demilune) in front of floor-to-ceiling shelves (topped with more books and a lamp) to break up the two-dimensionality.
- Set one or a pair of chairs in front of the shelves (holding, you guessed it, more books).
- Clip lights onto the shelves or add library lights at the top.
- Leave a shelf empty of books and put a bold object in it.
- Top the bookshelf with a collection of urns or baskets.

Candid Snapshots Don't discount your artless snapshots, consigning them to a drawer or leaving them floating alone in cyberspace. A "throwaway" picture taken at the end of a long, hot summer day when everyone is tired and sticky and happy stuck in a beautiful frame may contribute more than some stiff, formal picture. If you are the type who has proper, silver-framed portraits on tables, then you especially need a few candids around to loosen things up. Consider adding framed snaps alongside the wedding portraits or whatever you've got, or just pop a couple into the edge of a mirror or prop some on the mantel. I keep a bunch of snaps loose in a flattish bowl by the sofa for flipping through when I feel like it.

But go easy. The key is that the snapshots and family photos you display to the world should feel like talismans for you, and odd, cheerful treasures for your guests to stumble on. It is a little unseemly to overwhelm guests in your living areas with multitudinous scenes from your happy life. The more private the area of the house, the more it can handle personal pictures. Places like the bedroom or dressing area, and even bathrooms and hallways, are lovely places to load up on the family pix. (I once went to dinner at the home of a couple who had on display in the living room an enormous photo of themselves in a half-naked embrace. TMI!) Appropriateness is essential for good decorating—and good taste.

THIS IS HOW

Creating Order
Use similar frames
to unify a diverse
grouping of pictures.
This way even if some
are formal portraits,
some random snaps,
some in color, others
black-and-white,
and still others perhaps
the odd drawing or
love note, they will all
look as if they belong
together.

STYLE TIP
A good rule of
thumb is that
a sparsely furnished
room gets a sparing
dose of art, and the
more densely packed
the room, the
more pictures the
walls can handle.

Pictures and Ephemera

There is no reason to wait around until your budget allows you to buy "real" art. You can make little "nothings"— postcards, notes from friends, souvenir matchbooks, or beautiful party invitations—look terrific by giving them a special place or treatment. These mementos can also be mixed to great effect with good pieces of art. Decorator Miles Redd hangs "spin art" made from the old Mattel toy (his own DIY version of Abstract Expressionism) next to museum-quality art. I was completely charmed by the shells decorator Tom Scheerer glued to white paper and framed in a bedroom in his Bahamas house. I have seen wonderful bathrooms hung floor to ceiling with framed botanicals from pages of a book, and another plastered entirely with postcards. Look around and see what you've got.

Salon-Style Hanging 1. Work out your arrangement on the floor first.
2. Cut a paper template to the size of each picture.
3. Re-create your floor arrangement on the wall by taping up the paper templates.
4. When you've got it, start hammering.

Paintings and Drawings

A home really needs some paintings and drawings, but for those of us who are not shopping the Sotheby's Old Masters sales, there are many galleries and websites devoted to decently priced art and photography. And then there are charity auctions, secret meccas where artists' donated work can be nabbed for way under market value. Art-school exhibits are another good source, but even the professionals have started to get wise to this. The idea is to be surrounded by creativity and inspiration.

Picture trends cycle in and out of fashion just as anything decor related does. (Remember black-and-white photos on picture ledges?) Our own moment favors art hung all over the wall, often up to the ceiling. Hanging pictures "salon style," as this is called (after the way art was hung at the exhibitions at the Paris Salon in the nineteenth century), is great if you have a mixed bag of art because people pay attention to the overall effect rather than to the quality of any particular piece.

A sign of throwaway chic is not to hang pictures at all, but just to lean them against a wall atop a table or a mantel, or even against another picture. Art resting hither and thither creates an insouciant atmosphere that indicates "Things in this house are not static."

Not Too High: You should look down a bit on the lowest picture. About fifty-seven inches from the floor is an average height; repress the instinct to hang higher.

Not All Alone: Think less about where on the wall a picture goes, more about where it hangs in relation to the furniture or objects below it. Art needs to engage in a dialogue with the stuff near it. Otherwise you can end up with the common malady of picture-floating-sadly-in-a-sea-of-wall syndrome.

STYLE TIP
Collections of things should be low enough to be lived with and enjoyed, set out on tables, not stashed away high up on shelves or behind glass.

Tablescapes

The term "tablescape" is a coinage of the great English decorator (and zhuzher of objects nonpareil) David Hicks. No one could take a few things—cups, pencils, a box, a stack of books—and turn them into a tabletop composition as visually stunning and pleasing as great art as well as he could. Opposite is one of his tabletops from the 1970s. (And the one above is the current bedroom desk of his daughter, India.)

Tablescapes are made from what I like to call the "smalls" in a house—those precious little objects that are the grown-up versions of the toads and stones and broken sticks and bits of gathered string that we stuffed into our pockets as children. Nothing can add vitality to a room or clutter the hell out of it more than one's smalls.

The stern Sister Parish used to engage in a practice her employees termed "traying" in which she went around a new client's house with a tray scooping up all the ornaments, figurines, bibelots, and knickknacks she deemed superfluous. Tough, but necessary. If it's not beautiful, useful, or meaningful, you might as well lose it. And then the arranging can begin.

Decorators obsess over how to wield our decorative objets. On the frontlines of style, the tablescapers face off against the tchotchkeyites. The tablescaping aesthete believes in clustering like objects together to

create a strong visual statement, while the savvyless tchotchkeyite tends to disseminate objects all around the room, diminishing their impact and creating a sense of bitsyness.

So how do we group and arrange our beloved curiosities so that they form a tableau and not just a cluster of junk? The secret is this: when things are grouped together by a shared color, tone, material, or shape, no matter what they are, no matter how insignificant, no matter how different in other ways, they instantly become a worthy and vibrant little scene.

If it makes you feel any better, when you see a brilliant composition in a picture of a room in a magazine, know that it has probably been reworked about two hundred times. Even Hicks's were. "One of the most relaxing and pleasurable things in life, I think," he wrote, "is to rearrange one's books, one's pictures, and one's smaller possessions." Tableaux don't just happen, they are tweaked into existence.

Grouping Objects

Experiment with what works well in a grouping by gathering together on an empty table a load of small objects from all around your house—boxes, vases, bowls, candlesticks, shells, whatever you've got. Move them around to see how they relate to one other—"dialogue" with one another—and then start to group things.

Try:
- things with the same color but different textures
- things that share the same shape or material
- a monochrome grouping, maybe all white or all glass, perhaps even set off by silver or wood things
- like things, such as a collection of ceramic dogs or eggcups or toy boats grouped together

DELICIOUS
SCENT

I then filled the hall with the three things that
were essential to me in any room:
real candlelight, wood fires, and lovely flowers.

—NANCY LANCASTER

A unique part of each home is its scent, made up of a mixture of the life of the house and the fragrance we layer upon that. This is the first thing most people are aware of when they enter a home. Scent has the power to delight us and to remain with us in memory. As scent (both good and bad) has a profound relationship to our emotions about places and people, good scent is crucial to style, which itself ought to be an uplifting force. (Can a place ever be really stylish if it is musty or dank or harbors the olfactory history of meals long past?)

My ideal scent would be something like fresh air mixed with white flowers mixed with a burning fire and a little musky boxwood—all riding around on a breeze of lemon. My reality is often more like wet woolens and stinky socks. Creating a delicious and subtly palpable smell for our homes is not about spraying on some fragrance to cover over less savory smells. The key, rather, is to start with as fresh a base as possible before mixing in additional fragrances.

Previous pages:
Fresh air, flowers,
scented oil, a
wonderful view,
and a bubbly
bath—heaven!

Delicious-smelling Products

The background scents of our lives are made up of obvious things like coffee, supper, wood, dogs, books, children, and whatever drifts in through an open window. But they also come from what we use on our floors, clothes, and bodies.

Why use household cleansers that leave a chemical odor behind when many natural products have wonderfully fresh scents like citrus and geranium? (Having to scrub a little harder seems a price worth paying for having essential oils released into the air.)

The same goes for fresh-smelling detergents and linen sprays. It's not about perfuming your clothes and sheets but about infusing them with scent. Linen waters and sprays that can be used when ironing or spritzed onto folded sheets before storing them are a necessary indulgence. Well, maybe not necessary, but a whiff of fresh, lavender-infused sheets is a sensory delight when I open the closet or climb into bed.

Knowing that all the bath salts and oils and body lotions and soaps we use factor directly into the scent of our home is all the incentive I need to indulge in my favorite (often terribly expensive) aromatic beauty products. That, and the fact that they affect my mood and outlook so powerfully. If you only allow yourself one luxurious indulgence, make it your signature. When I (sparingly) dab on some of my favorite seventy-five-dollar body milk from Santa Maria Novella, and my daughter oohs and aahs over how wonderful I smell, I think about how this sensation may be rooting deep into her memory.

For me, part of creating a wonderful-smelling home is about wanting it to be something lovely my children recall after they've left childhood behind.

NICE TO KNOW

It is nice for the fragrance in rooms to follow the arc of the seasons.
Spring and Summer: Flowers and the sea, mint, lemon, grapefruit, white flowers like lily of the valley and honeysuckle
Winter: Fire and the forest—musks, juniper, fig, clove, rosemary
Year-Round: The mood-lifting scent of lavender—in candles, linen waters, sachets, bath oils, and laundry soaps

Potpourri When a super stylish friend brought me a gift of a speckle-painted ceramic bowl and a baggie of potpourri to go in it I thought she was kidding. To me this stuff was the very definition of adding stink on stink. I knew only the mall version: desiccated rose petals with crusty orange rinds emitting some kind of artificial vanilla odor. But what Rita introduced me to was wholly different. Made by Santa Maria Novella, this singular mixture has a slightly spicy, musky smell like an Italian cypress wood.

Since my conversion, I have never been without this particular potpourri (although I'm sure there must be others as good). There are always bowls of it around the house, but especially in the front hall, where its perfume greets me every time I return home. (A little fluffing or gentle crushing of its leaves releases the fragrance when you need an extra jolt. And when it dries out, you have to top it off or toss it.)

Scented Candles

While candles are not the self-service fragrance that potpourri is, since you have to be home to light them, they do allow you to manage the fragrance of your home and to change it up room by room and season by season. They can light up the mantel, a bathroom, a windowsill, or a table—pretty much anywhere except the dining table, which should be reserved for the smell of supper, not perfume.

The big issue with scented candles is that one person's aromatherapy may be another's olfactory torture. But if you limit yourself to high-quality candles and products from companies devoted to the art of fragrance, you'll be far more likely to find consensus among noses.

Favorite Purveyors of Fragrance

I've listed some of my favorite products, although probably no one else will have the same preferences. But you can trust me on finding something you love from these sources.

- Cire Trudon, the oldest Parisian candlemaker. Pondicherry candle.
- Santa Maria Novella, the legendary Florentine apothecary. Pomegranate candle and soap and the terra-cotta pomegranate infused with pomegranate oil, stashed in a linen closet; their musk shampoo (for men and women).
- Miller Harris, young English nose Lyn Harris's line. Figue Amère candle.

- Jo Malone, some of the crispest, clearest scents available and great for layering one with another. (The Verbenas of Provence perfume doubles as a fresh room spray for linens and upholstery.)
- Diptyque, the candlemaker of choice for the fashion set. I use their waxed soap-like bars for scenting closets and drawers.

Flowers The thought of arranging flowers can unhinge even the most stylish people. The secret to "doing" flowers is not to be intimidated. You are the boss of them! You can whack the long stems off roses so just their flowery heads peek over the vase or cut a flowering plant and turn it into fodder for the vase. You can do whatever you want, and then redo it the next time if it doesn't work. And anyway, sometimes the chicest thing is just to drop a bunch of flowers like some daisies or sweet peas in a jam jar and call it a day.

I love the way white and green flowers pick up on the white and green pottery and boxes on my mantel, but I also am crazy for how bright-pink flowers shock against my dull-green velvet-covered table. In addition, I have certain vases that I know look good in certain areas. When something works, don't be afraid to keep doing it over and over again. A style signature is not a lack of imagination; it's the definition of one!

Flowers on the Cheap

Fancy flower shops? Not necessary. No farmers' market? No problem. You can get decent flowers from the supermarket year-round, rarely spending more than twenty pounds a fortnight. Here's how:

- Before you buy, decide what vase the flowers will work in and where you'll put them.
- Flowers are least costly (and most delightful) in their natural flowering season. So tulips in May and peonies in June, not in February.
- Buy flowering plants when you can, like hyacinths, paperwhites, and amaryllis, which last much longer than cut flowers, and drop them in a cachepot.
- Go for the impact of scale with a few large branches or giant tropical leaves.

STYLE TIP
Choose flowers and
their vases in hues
that either mimic or
boldly contrast with
colors in the room,
and watch your
flowers magically
integrate themselves
into your decorative
scheme.

Arranging Flowers
Think about a mixed bouquet as three elements—the filler, the flowers, and the wispy bits. These ingredients build an arrangement.

1) *The filler* is the foundation: the leafy, branchy stuff that fills the vase and forms the base.

2) *The flowers,* like daisies, dahlias, tulips, and roses, are the stars, the main attraction.

3) *The wispy bits* are the taller, stalkier, grassier things that rise out of the arrangement and loosen it up.

Four Basic Vases

Flared Vases
Vases that widen at the top are lovely for loose bunches of wildflowers or for flowers like tulips that naturally bend over the vase. When you have ramrod-straight flowers, like long-stemmed roses, they tend to fall to the edges of the vase, leaving an empty center. A string or rubber band around the stems can control the splay.

Cachepots
These pretty decorative containers may seem a little old-ladyish, but they are wildly useful. You can obscure an ugly plastic pot by simply dropping it right in— hence the French meaning of the word: hide pot.

Pinched-top Vases
Vases that are slightly tighter at the lip, like most pitchers are, seem to magically "gather" the flowers into an arrangement on their own.

Bud Vases
You can't get much simpler than a container that holds one stem, or three. (Odd numbers look most natural.)

Gardeny Plants For someone who hates houseplants, I seem to have quite a lot of them. They really do establish a homey, well-tended feeling in a room. The key is having plants that look as if they've just come in from the garden rather than those dreary leafy things, like spider plants and philodendron, that seem to belong in a classroom.

It's really nice to have blooming bulbs and flowers in the dead of winter. Things like lemon trees and those unfairly maligned geraniums, particularly the scented varieties, are wonderful reminders of sunnier days. Plants ought to anticipate the passing of winter and the coming of spring, the way potted bulbs do, not just sit there doing the same thing (i.e., nothing) all year round. The reason those classroom plants are in the classroom is that they thrive on neglect.

Growing flowering plants or nice topiaries indoors is much trickier, so you have to be prepared for failure. Tender, more sensitive plants give way to bugs or desiccation or just go dormant, and you must be firm. If you don't have a garden to nurse them or a basement for them to sit out their dormancy, man up and toss them. You do not want to end up living in a hopeless plant hospital. Style counts; a bit of photosynthesis doesn't.

Nice Plants

If you don't have your own garden to cull from, you can buy some lovely things in flower shops, such as:

- sweet-scented jasmine
- a big pot of rosemary
- clipped balls of myrtle
- bulbs like amaryllis or daffodils or paperwhites
- cyclamen
- velthemia
- geraniums
- citrus trees

A SENSE OF
HISTORY

Houses of the best taste are like clothes
of the best tailors—it takes
their age to show us how good they are.

—HENRY JAMES

n our homes, we get to shut the door on the outside world, yet for a home to feel alive it has to have a strong decorative connection to that very world. Decorating gives us an opportunity to make that connection, surrounding ourselves with objects we appreciate from diverse cultures, traditions, and even periods.

Pieces with a bit of history—made by hand or old or steeped in other traditions—often carry the marks of age on their surfaces, indicators of use and love. Our furniture, rugs, and fabrics get richer and more beautiful with age.

Previous pages: In Caroline Irving's house in Springs, New York, a Directoire sofa, an antique mirror, a Persian rug, and a suzani brought back from Uzbekistan import a worldly vibe.

On an existential level, this fading of fabric, dulling of colors, and softening of woods points to a sad truth: time passes and nothing lasts forever. Yet that's precisely what makes a house feel more poignant, placing it in the flow of life. For a home to be vibrant and truly stylish, it needs to be open to the real world—its (far-flung) treasures and its (own) temporality.

Ethnic Textiles While I have touted ethnic and old fabrics else-where because of the cozy richness their pattern can add to a room (see the Cozifications chapter), handcrafted textiles also bring a worldliness to a home. Given the globalization of practically everything, it is amazing that traditional textiles are still woven by hand in styles and techniques used for centuries. Some of my personal favorites for decorating include Central Asian suzanis and ikats, Indonesian and West African batiks, Moroccan wedding blankets, and American quilts.

We are quite lucky to be able to gather these far-flung treasures in our homes. Since every room can handle a wonderful piece of fabric, when love strikes, buy it. You can always figure out what to do with it later.

Put It Here: Ethnic Textiles
- Use on a bed as a coverlet
- Hang on a wall
- Fold over an upholstered headboard
- Drape over a table
- Hang over the back of a chair or a sofa
- Make into pillows or curtains
- Upholster a chair or a bench

Pottery and Crafts

I love a sinuous molded plastic Panton chair or a crisply cornered Parsons table as much as the next girl, but machine-made forms in a room need to be balanced with the humanity of things imperfectly formed, things crafted by hand. Hand-thrown ceramics, for instance, always reveal the human touch, which infuses them with charm.

I am not suggesting we go all "craft fair" with the hanging macramé baskets or the earth-toned drip-glazed coffee mugs of our primary school teachers. But there are so many artists, artisans, and craftspeople toiling away making the world more interesting and beautiful to look at. And craft fairs and sites like Etsy.com, as well as artists' and potters' studios, curated shops, and art-school graduation shows, are resources that can help add originality and humanity to our homes.

One Good Antique

Every room needs at least one good antique to lend it a sense of stability. Rooms seem sort of flighty or unsophisticated without one fine, sturdy piece hanging around giving them some old-world gravitas. Quality pieces carry a story with them, speaking of the place and time in which they were made.

Antiques are simply better made than most new pieces (they've lasted this long), and their craftsmanship shows. But if you are like me and no one has seen fit to leave you any antiques, you're just going to have to decide whether this is the kind of investment that makes sense to you. (You know what I think.) The good news is that quite often a really good old piece costs less than decent new furniture—which can be crazy expensive. (Even a 1920s repro of a French chair, which almost qualifies as an antique, is far superior to a mass-produced new one—and usually cheaper.) In nearly every city, there are wonderful antiques shops that straddle that delightful middle ground between junk shops and those terrifying places that cater to the top .01 percent.

Faded Rugs Whole books can be (and have been) written about rugs. In terms of carpets as cozifiers, I just want to address their color and pattern. Big statement rugs with bright colors or bold designs that shout at you when you walk into a room, demanding your attention, are not cozifiers. Cozifiers blend. A rug must weave itself (pardon the pun) more seamlessly into a room for maximum cozification. I love old or faded rugs—like striped Indian dhurries, pale pastel Turkish Oushaks, or mellowed golden Persian carpets—for the subtle way they add depth and texture.

A rug can be a starting point for a room's palette, inspiring wall and fabric colors, or you can choose one to pick up on colors you've already got going on. In either case, the more you choose to feature the rug's less obvious colors elsewhere, the more subtly it will be layered into the room. For instance, a delicate light gray on the edge of a rug featuring many other colors in its design can be accented with gray lamps or lampshades.

How Big Should Your Rug Be?
Pay attention here, this is confusing!

If your furniture is on the rug: Allow one or two feet from the wall to the edge of the rug.

(Basically, your deepest piece is only off the rug one inch.)

If your furniture is off the rug: Measure your deepest piece of furniture (probably a sofa), and then add one inch to that number and allow that much distance from the wall to the edge of the rug.

If your room is small: Keep all furniture on the rug, and leave no more than one foot from the wall to the edge of the carpet. (The idea here is to go as big as you can, and not to break up the room visually.)

Old Things If you've got one fine antique, it's still not okay for everything else to be brand-spanking new (e.g., one piece speaking of, say, Spain in the nineteenth century and everything else speaking of China in the twenty-first!). Even modernists need some old junk hanging around. If nearly everything hails from the here and now, a place will feel hermetic or cartoony, closed off from the world.

This is just about gathering some old stuff, not anything particularly fancy. It could be old books, ceramics, glassware, linens, vases, rugs—anything. Even a ratty old table that's not in great condition but has beautiful legs or an interesting shape can be rehabbed with some black or white paint and make a striking contribution to a room. These things are not usually looked for, but rather just found—in shops, on your travels, or even in the street—and they are often unique. And isn't it nice to have things that you won't find in someone else's house?

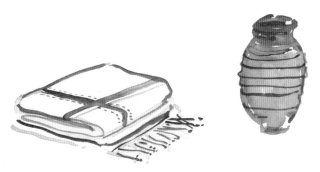

Patina Patina happens. It is the history a piece wears on its sleeve, what Billy Baldwin referred to as the "mellow charm" of a lovely old object. A home needs some of the softness of old wood, the dullness of aged metal, the subtle colors of an original paint job, or fabric faded by the sun. Without a little of this, a house feels cold and untouched by human life.

Fancy old Sibyl Colefax, cofounder of the posh English decorating house Colefax and Fowler, used to "bash about" her fabrics, washing new chintzes in tea to dull the colors and dragging sofa covers outside to be rained on and faded by the sun. Not much different from buying pre-washed (acid-washed, stonewashed, hammer-beaten, whatever) denim. In fact, many new fabrics now tout their wrinkly, faded, or otherwise intentionally imperfect "vintage" style. A little decrepitude can be just the thing for some fabrics and rugs and furniture. But then again, I also like people marked by age and experience.

Of course, patina just happens from living. Life is messy and gloriously imperfect, and some signs of wear and tear indicate a well-loved, well-used home.

I have a pale, whitish interior and small children who have been taught to respect furniture and objects, to not eat on the sofa or track mud onto the carpets. But it's also their house and they're free to arrive onto the sofa from a running leap or to build forts with its cushions. If that means a bit of fraying or nicking, I say bring it on. I fear a pristine life more than I fear scuff marks on the floor. In fact, they remind me of kids joyously skateboarding across the living room and guests tromping about.

Everybody's threshold for patina is different, but don't try to clean and buff away a piece's history. Think of a bit of wear as a celebration of your experience. These are our marks, our scars, our lives—our perfectly imperfect homes.

ILLUSTRATION
INDEX

ROOM INDEX

The illustrations in this book owe a great debt to the people who created the homes that inspired them. Some watercolors are fairly faithful to the original rooms and others more loosely based. With thanks— and apologies for liberties taken—to the designers whose rooms I love.

NICE LIGHTING

page 21
Inspired by a room designed by Jeffrey Bilhuber.
The rough basket stands in contrast
to the fine console, lamps, and mirror.

INTRODUCTION

page 13
On the mantel at the Hunting Lodge, Nicky Haslam's
country house, he mixes snapshots and
party invites among china and silver candlesticks.

page 23
Tom Scheerer used a yellow ceramic lamp as
the focal point of a tablescape that
includes a ceramic tile and a porcelain hand.

page 26
Inspired by a room designed by Jeffrey Bilhuber
from his book *Defining Luxury*.

page 31
An overscaled antique lantern hangs over
a quilt-covered, book-laden table in
Janet de Botton's house in the South of France.

page 28
In his Manhattan town house, Miles Redd matched
the silk shades to his red velvet sofa,
as well as to bits of red in the art and cushions.

A PROPER WELCOME

page 35
In a city entry hall, Markham Roberts
set striped wallpaper at juxtaposing angles
on each wall for a dramatic effect.

page 36
The hallway in James de Givenchy's Bahamas house decorated by Tom Scheerer boasts hats on hooks and towels and beach mats in baskets for a quick exit to the beach.

page 39
For this front hall in Nashville, David Netto created a lovely tableau on the console, as well as a fabric-covered central table for flowers, keys, and bags.

page 37
The hallway in Scheerer's own home in the Bahamas has a nautical-seeming mirror, framed maps of the island, a local conch shell, and a beachy glass bottle lamp.

page 41
In John Stefanidis's mudroom in the English countryside, hats and scarves are at the ready for guests, as are walking sticks, umbrellas, and boots in all sizes stashed in a cupboard.

PLACES FOR CHATTING

page 47
Blue-striped slipcovers on the furniture
in John Stefanidis's country
house keep it feeling cool in summer.

page 52
Arranged for intimate chatting: two closely
placed sofas in Nicky Haslam's sitting
room in the country share a book-covered
ottoman and a pair of slipper chairs.

page 49
In this room with aubergine-lacquered walls,
David Netto designed plenty of comfortable
seating options in addition to
a secondary seating area around a table.

page 57
In the drawing room of the Brooklyn home of
artists Hugo Guinness and Elliott Puckette,
Guinness's own botanicals climb the walls above
a small sofa nestled into a corner.

page 58
Miles Redd accommodates many
possible social situations with one seating
arrangement. Note how the chairs
seem to be in conversation with one another.

page 64
In a tiny Manhattan apartment with
a minuscule front hall, Rita Konig's lamp
often did double duty as a hat rack.

A BIT OF QUIRK

page 63
Tom Scheerer's symmetrical but unusual
composition of prints and sconces hangs above
a Victorian sofa with a strong personality.

page 65
In Nancy Lancaster's cottage, Little Haseley,
favorite family photos are stuffed hodgepodge
into the frame of an antique mirror.

SPOTS FOR BOOKS, DRINKS, & FEET

page 77
A large ottoman from Robert Kime acts
as both seat and coffee table in the living room
of Carolina Irving's New York apartment.

The talismanlike LOVE poster in Rita Konig's
apartment seems to broadcast good vibes
into the room.

page 67
The talismanlike LOVE poster in Rita Konig's
apartment seems to broadcast good vibes
into the room.

page 72
In the home of Nathalie and Amir Farman-Farma,
David Netto ensured that the scale of
the windows dominates the room by accentuating
their height with an enormous palm.

page 79
In a fabric-covered room in a Paris apartment
decorated by Lisa Fine, two small
occasional tables act as a coffee table.

page 81
In front of an end table holding decorative
objects, Jeffrey Bilhuber graciously layered two
smaller tables to hold objects in heavier rotation.

page 88
In Michael Smith's Los Angeles house, a
needlepoint pillow and wool Hermès blanket sit
atop a chair covered in a Bennison chintz.

COZIFICATIONS

page 87
Marella Agnelli's winter garden room in Marrakesh
is loaded up with cushions and two wicker
chairs that sit so close by that they're practically
snuggling the banquette.

page 89
The pale blues and beiges in this room
by Miles Redd are given some
weight by the addition of some inky black in
the cushions, lamp, and picture frames.

page 90
A tableau including a turquoise lamp, worry beads, and a plate by Teddy Millington Drake sit on a table covered with an Indonesian ikat fabric in John Stefanidis's house in Greece.

A DOTED-ON BEDROOM

page 101
In this bedroom designed by Jacques Grange, the wallpaper (Rayure Fleurie) and rug (Carrelage Castaing) are Madeleine Castaing designs, sold through Clarence House.

page 92
In Miles Redd's work, one can find examples of "the law of threes": the red of the chair is picked up in the pillow, lamps, rug, and even the flowers.

page 103
Rita Konig's New York bedroom feels remarkably un-urban with its heart-covered sheets, vining wallpaper, and leafy view.

page 105
The guest room in Kate and Andy Spade's
New York apartment has a matching
toile fabric on the walls and bedspread.

page 108
Inspired by jewelry designer Temple St. Clair's
New York bedroom, which features charmingly
mismatched pillows and suzani bedcover.

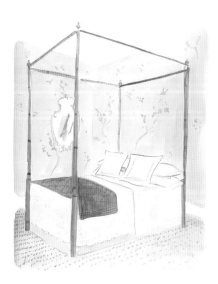

page 107
Inspired by a bedroom Peter Dunham
created for a decorator show house.

page 114
My bedroom in upstate New York,
decorated by Rita Konig.

page 117
Pierre Bergé's elegant bedroom
with leopard carpet at Hotel Lutetia,
designed by Jacques Grange.

page 123
Custom-colored Mauny wallpaper and an old
wood table add a sense of roominess to clothing
designer Rachel Riley's master bath.

page 118
The view over Albert Hadley's
bed toward the table, screen, and window
in his New York apartment.

page 124
Carolina Herrera Jr.'s bath in the Spanish
countryside is large and sparsely furnished: tub,
table, chair, and killer view.

page 127
Adapted from a beautifully tiled
bathroom by Michael Smith.

page 134
A bathroom in the apartment of Kate and Andy
Spade features Scalamandré's famous zebra
wallpaper and a boldly striped shower curtain.

page 129
Mica Ertegun's dressing table in Southampton,
New York. Tables draped with fabric,
like this Turkish cloth, are more often used in
bedrooms than in bathrooms.

GLAMIFICATIONS

page 139
High drama by Miles Redd: chinoiserie paper, silk
curtains, a crystal chandelier, gold chairs, leopard
fabric—kept under control by a tight color palette.

page 141
Charlotte Moss's study is a festival of pattern: robin's egg blue stenciled walls, red paisley-striped upholstery, fashion photographs and drawings, and books everywhere.

page 143
The deeply lacquered green entry hall in the West Village New York town house of Steven Gambrel.

page 142
Shocking peony-pink walls are almost all the decoration this room in Florida by John Stefanidis needs (yet it gets some Jansen chairs and a shell mirror from the '60s too).

page 144
For maximum reflective glamour, David Netto placed a starburst mirror above the console and a framed mirror on the floor under it.

page 146
The floor-to-ceiling mirrored panel in
a former apartment of fashion icon
Inès de La Fressange acts like another window.

page 149
Jenna Lyons and Vincent Mazeau hung
an antique crystal chandelier in the otherwise
modern and minimalist dining
room of their New York City town house.

page 147
A large stucco mirror from the '40s
dominates a wall in a New York apartment
designed by Jacques Grange.

page 151
A scene based on a writing table in the
home of Allison Sarofim.

page 153
Miles Redd's bedroom is a textural feast:
a mirrored four-poster bed hung with
a rich striped silk, made up with smooth cotton
sheets, and topped with a fur throw.

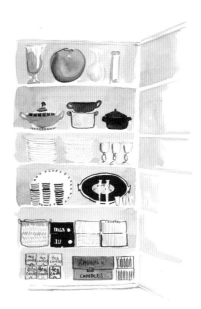

page 159
The well-composed shelves in Bunny Williams's
pantry are laden with hurricanes,
platters, planters, and plenty of candles.

DINNERS WITH
FRIENDS

page 157
John Stefanidis sets an outdoor table
with indoor finery in the shade of lindens:
crisp linen, silver, and glass.

page 160
Miles Redd's drinks table is always at the ready
in a corner of his living room. Before a party, ice,
lemons, flowers, and some candlelight are added.

page 162
Tea by the fire in Colefax and Fowler's Roger
Banks-Pye's country house, where he was after
a look that was "cozy, warm, and rather shabby."

page 167
Carolyne Roehm loves mixing various hues of blue
in table settings and decor so much, she devoted
an entire book to it: *A Passion for Blue and White*.

page 165
Tom Scheerer often mixes Saarinen tables into
his rooms as side tables, end tables, and
here as a dining table/coffee table, set for a buffet.

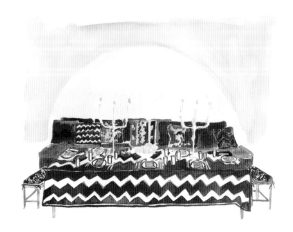

page 169
Liberties were taken with this illustration based on
John Stefanidis's house on Patmos: his
tablecloth was, and probably always is, white linen.

A PERSONAL
NARRATIVE

page 179
Shelves in the home of stylist Lili Diallo, where
books mingle with objects in black and white.

page 182
In a guest room in Tom Scheerer's Harbor
Island house, he made art from shells
collected on the beach, glued onto paper,
and put in simple plastic frames.

page 180
Rita Konig taped black-and-white snapshots of
friends taken with an old Polaroid Land camera on
the wall above the mantel in her living room.

page 184
Framed pictures climb the stair walls in the home
of Jason Nixon and John Loecke.

page 185
This off-center arrangement of pictures
by Jeffrey Bilhuber is balanced thanks to an equal
amount of space between the frames.

page 187
David Hicks always chose objects for a table that
relate in color, shape, and/or texture. Here
they all take their lead from the lamp on the table.

page 186
India Hicks, daughter of famed designer
David Hicks, seems to have "tablescaping" in her
blood: the objects on her bedroom desk,
including boxes, books, glasses, and personal
mementos, are all artfully composed.

DELICIOUS SCENT

page 190
Inspired by Nina Campbell's lovely
London bathroom, but with a big window
added looking onto her garden.

page 193
In this Connecticut front hall designed by Jeffrey
Bilhuber, large branches of juniper and
pots of lavender and rosemary bring the fresh
scent of the outdoors into the house.

page 205
In India Hicks's Harbor Island sitting room,
pictures from her family, antique wooden toys and
boxes collected by her husband, and roller
skates under a side table left by her daughter
speak of her history, past and present.

page 199
The Indian room in John Stefanidis's country
house took its name from the hot pink of
the sofa. He even matched the flowers, here
bougainvillea, to the scheme.

page 207
In Kathryn Ireland's Santa Monica pattern-on-
pattern bedroom, antique fabrics mix with fabrics
of her design and those designed by others.

page 209
Frédéric Méchiche's apartment in the Marais
district of Paris is a minimalist loft but
of a style where a Bertoia chair from the '60s
resides alongside an eighteenth-century
mirror and a Mapplethorpe photograph.

FABRIC INDEX

Most fabric designs start as
sketches or watercolors, but these
are watercolors Virginia Johnson
made from existing fabrics.

page 211
Inspired by Bunny Williams and John Rosselli's
grand sitting room in the Dominican Republic with its
harmony of pales coming from the Indian dhurrie,
painted panels, plaster mirror, and gorgeous textiles.

The endpapers are sketches of John Stefanidis's
Zanzibar fabric/stefanidisfabrics.com.

page 11
Fanfare by John Stefanidis/stefanidisfabrics.com.

page 12
Bells by John Stefanidis from his Passepartout
Collection/stefanidisfabrics.com.

page 17
Petite Zig Zag by Alan Campbell/
quadrillefabrics.com.

pages 215, 237
Lemon Tree, a fabric design by Virginia Johnson/
Virginiajohnson.com.

RESOURCES

STORE LISTINGS

A very biased and not comprehensive resource list of some favorite artisans, antiques shops, e-commerce sites, fabric houses, and large emporiums.

ABC Home is a vast, multilevel store located just north of Union Square that carries a well-curated and worldly collection of goods. It is best to visit this shop in person, as the scope of their website is rather limited, and part of the joy (and expense) is getting swept into their carefully constructed world. Owner Paulette Cole also sources as many environmentally and socially conscious goods as possible. *888 & 881 Broadway, New York, NY 10003* **abchome.com**

Aero Studios has owner/designer Thomas O'Brien's signature American aesthetic all over it. Displaying his various furniture and tabletop collaborations, the store also carries one-of-a-kind pieces that O'Brien has picked up from various locales around the world. A must-see as opposed to a web browse. *419 Broome Street, New York, NY 10013* **aerostudios.com**

Alfies Antiques Market is London's largest indoor market for antiques, collectables, and all things vintage. You can spend many a happy hour here browsing among the varied stalls and chatting to the owners, who are a font of specialist knowledge. **allfiesantiques.com**

Andrianna Shamaris's SoHo boutique boasts a decidedly organic collection of Eastern wares. While carrying ikat textiles and objets d'art, the store specializes in beautiful and varied wood furnishings that the owner discovers on her travels or designs herself. Shamaris has a relatively thorough website of her modern yet earthy offerings. *121 Greene Street, New York, NY 10012* **andriannashamarisinc.com**

Anthropologie channels a youthful, wanderlust-like aesthetic that is bright and Bohemian. For a chain store, they offer a surprisingly independent and often quirky assortment of accessories, furnishings, and tabletop items. Good prices and an easily navigable website make the store a reliable spot to find something that feels unique. **anthropologie.com**

Antique Designs Ltd offer modern versions of antique linens for the bedroom and table. Antique fabrics are becoming harder to source, and these modern ones in traditional designs, with drawn threadwork and embroidery as optional embellishments, are a real find. **antique-designs.co.uk**

Antony Todd's Greenwich Village store is more of a gallery than a shop. Todd's meticulous eye ensures a bevy of beautiful objects, though at a price. Whether you buy or not, his perfectly edited space is worth a trip, for inspiration or otherwise. *44 East 11th Street, New York, NY 10003* **antonytodd.com**

Astier de Villatte's handmade, chic tableware has redefined the classic, boring white plate. This Parisian manufacturer has a website featuring their various styles; however, Astier de Villatte is only found at certain specialty stores in the U.S. As each piece is handmade, prices aren't low. **astierdevillatte.com**

Beall & Bell, located on the North Fork of Long Island, has specialized in the found object for the past seventeen years. The owners scour flea markets and auction houses alike for a fantastic mélange of furniture and accessories, ranging from French, English, and American antiques to industrial and midcentury-modern pieces. Though they have a website, Beall & Bell is well worth a trip. **beallandbell.com**

Bell'Invito, a couture stationer and letterpress printer, was founded by a former Neiman Marcus art director with a background in graphic design. Specializing in beautifully lined envelopes and social stationery, Bell'Invito offers custom invitations for weddings and events that are expansive and elegant. **bellinvito.com**

Blackman Cruz, located in a sprawling space on Highland Avenue in Los Angeles, specializes in the dramatic. Without a binding design ethos, the showroom's furnishings cultivate a cinematic style that spans time and continents. Owners Adam Blackman and David Cruz have parlayed their unique aesthetic into their own line of designs, BC Workshop, and have collaborated with various artists, making the store an amalgam of old and new. Blackman Cruz boasts a thorough website. **blackmancruz.com**

Brent and Becky's Bulbs offers a large and exhaustive range of bulbs, from the popular and common to the little known and hard to find. This Virginia-based nursery has a website replete with their seasonal offerings and is a great resource for horticulture information. **brentandbeckysbulbs.com**

Calypso Home channels the fashion brand tropical-island-by-way-of-Paris aesthetic, showcasing graphic dhurrie-covered poufs, fine linens, and objets d'art. Though some of the store's pieces are available on the web, it is best to visit one of the store's locations. **calypsostbarth.com**

Christopher Spitzmiller has created a signature style with his collection of gourd-style lamps. His handmade, ceramic lamps come in a variety of shapes and finishes, from the simple to the ornate. While his work has been knocked off and similar lamps can be had a lot cheaper, if you can afford it, his are exquisitely made, perfectly proportioned, and will last a lifetime. A sampling of styles is available on his website, and Spitzmiller's work is sold through specialty stores and showrooms across the U.S. **christopherspitzmiller.com**

Circa Lighting has a wide range of classic lighting of every kind and collaborates with designers such as Alexa Hampton, Thomas O'Brien, and Michael Smith. They sell through shops around the country. **circalighting.com**

Cire Trudon, France's oldest and most distinguished candlemaker with an exquisite, century-old shop in Paris's Left Bank, has recently set up a chic outpost on New York's Bowery. With offerings of pillars in every hue to simple tapers, the company has become recognized for its eighteenth- and nineteenth-century-style bust candles in the form of Marie Antoinette and Napoléon. I adore their Pondicherry candle—and when done, the label and wax come off easily, leaving a lovely green glass vase for flowers. Their simple luxe-meets-industrial boutique merits a visit. **ciretrudon.com**

Cole & Son have been producing wallpapers in north London since 1875, and still employ traditional techniques, such as block printing, screen printing, and flocking for custom designs. They draw from their unique historical archive to produce stunning modern collections. **cole-and-son.com**

Comptoir de Famille is a wholesale distributor of classic French country furnishings and accessories, though their specialty is tableware and linens. Check their website for vendors. **comptoir-de-famille.com**

The Conran Shop has branched out from its home in the iconic Michelin building in London's Chelsea to a world-wide concern, with stores in New York and Japan. Its furniture range is unsurpassed, with vintage pieces sitting alongside modern gems, and its roster of designer names keep it at the leading edge of home design. **conranshop.co.uk**

D. Porthault, the signature Parisian designer of fine linens, offers sheets, towels, and linens that range from the color saturated to the refined and understated. Their cocktail napkins make a costly but superfine wedding gift. The website shows a complete range of patterns and styles. *470 Park Avenue, New York, NY 10022* **dporthaultparis.com**

Dash & Albert carries an assortment of classic wool and cotton rugs, from ticking stripe and herringbone patterns to more graphic, Eastern designs at really amazing prices. They also carry a range of outdoor rugs that would work equally well indoors. They have a thorough website and are stocked throughout the U.S. **dashandalbert.com**

Designers Guild was the creation of British designer Tricia Guild, and her distinctive designs display a wild exuberance that take florals as their inspiration, but are never twee. Fabrics for furniture and window treatments, wallpapers, floor coverings, and furniture are all available through their own showrooms and homewares stores worldwide. **designersguild.com**

Dwell Studios' Christiane Lemieux spins her love for midcentury modern style into a playful line of linens and home accessories and baby things. Prints range from the naïve to the sophisticated, typically in muted tones with a nod to geometric patterns. **dwellstudio.com**

Farrow & Ball are renowned for their extensive array of shades of white paint, but they also produce wonderfully deep shades that always look amazing on walls, due to their excellent quality. A range of wallpapers complements their paint tones. **farrow-ball.com**

Few and Far is the creative outlet of Priscilla Carluccio. Seasonal collections of clothing and jewelry jostle for space with toys and home accessories, sourced and chosen from India, Morocco, France, Italy, and the UK. **fewandfar.net**

Flamant, based in Belgium, manufactures a wide variety of home goods, from furniture and accessories to paint and textiles, which range from the independently designed to reproductions, particularly Gustavian, Louis XVI, and industrial. They have stores throughout Europe and one in Iowa. **flamant.com**

Frances Palmer is a masterful potter who creates classically shaped vases with a quirky feel. Her studio line provides beautiful basic tabletop designs at a much lower price than her custom pieces. Styles are available on her website. One of my favorite wedding-gift sources. **francespalmerpottery.com**

Galerie des Lampes is a French lighting manufacturer and antique lighting dealer used by the fanciest of French decorators. They specialize in classically shaped lamps, sconces, and fixtures that are customizable and sold through specialty stores and showrooms. **galeriedeslampes.com**

Gingerlily, a British manufacturer of silk bedding, offers an array of fine silk linens for the bedroom. I love them for their slender silk (rather than down) filled comforters, which keep you warm without being bulky. These are the paradigm-shifters of comforters, introduced to me by Rita Konig. Their goods are sold exclusively in the U.K. and in Europe. **gingerlily.co.uk**

Guinevere has a wonderful shop on London's King's Road selling a tempting selection of antiques. Their textiles are especially good,

including antique dhurries and cotton bedspreads from India, with very good smart French linens. **guinevere.co.uk**

Hable Construction, the fabric and accessories line created by sisters Katharine and Susan Hable, has become known for its durable and charming printed canvas bags and spunky pillows, which are available on the website. Their designs are graphically oriented and geometrically whimsical. Hable also has a line of to-the-trade-only fabrics, which are sold through Holland & Sherry. **hableconstruction.com**

Heath Ceramics, one of the few midcentury American potters remaining in business, produces a range of clean and classic tableware in a variety of colors. Simplicity reigns supreme in their designs, and a handcrafted feel sets their dishes and tiles apart. **heathceramics.com**

Henry Dean, a Belgian designer of exquisite glassware, offers a line of handblown, elegantly simple glasses in a range of shapes, sizes, and colors. Love the drinking glasses and the hurricane lanterns. His pieces are available at specialty stores and to the trade. **henrydean.be**

Hollywood at Home, English-born, L.A.-based decorator Peter Dunham's La Cienega Boulevard store, offers everything from his custom-designed furniture and textiles and those of his like-minded friends Caroline Irving and Kathryn Ireland to vintage pieces and antiques. The shop reflects an appreciation of styles from California to the Middle East, which makes it a great resource. *724 North La Cienega Boulevard, Los Angeles, CA 90069* **hollywoodathome.com**

Ian Mankin produces a range of classic and organic cotton and linen fabrics in natural colourways, with stripes, including mattress ticking, checks, and plains their speciality. All the fabrics are available by the metre, as well as made up into cushions and furniture coverings. **ianmankin.co.uk**

Jamali Garden is the perfect source for floral and party supplies. They carry everything from decorative branches, votives, vases, and ribbon to faux silver julep cups and giant urns. Inexpensive and packed with decorative objects, Jamali is also fun to visit. *149 West 28th Street, New York, NY 10001* **jamaligarden.com**

Jane Sacchi sources antique linens and hemp from France, and offers an ever-changing selection of superb quality bed and table linen, which can be dyed or monogrammed to order. Toile de Jouy and toile de Nantes are her recent passions. **janesacchi.com**

John Cullen Lighting's design director Sally Storey brings her architectural background to bear on her lighting designs for homes and outdoor spaces. The company also produces a growing number of lighting products. **johncullenlighitng.co.uk**

John Derian gained his fame through his eponymous Victorian-nostalgia decoupage trays, but his East Village shop, now split into two stores, is much more. Dry Goods is filled with fine linens and Indian textiles, while John Derian Company boasts his mainstays along with other refined and independent designer tabletop items, art, and accessories. A favorite of the fashion set, and for good reason, there is little in his shops that I wouldn't be happy to take home! **johnderian.com**

John Robshaw's name has become synonymous with Indian textiles. His vibrant designs range from simple and sweet to bold and punchy across his linen, decorative pillow, and dhurrie lines. Robshaw has a thorough website and is stocked nationally at specialty stores. Every home can use some John Robshaw! **johnrobshaw.com**

Jonathan Adler, who launched his career as a potter, channels his love for midcentury-modern and happy design in his now large line of home goods, from tabletop to upholstery and everything in between. Bright, geometric patterns and a nod to irreverence make Adler's designs joyful and easily recognizable. His website is thorough and always as wonderful as he is himself. **jonathanadler.com**

Juliska's classically Belgian glassware, ceramics, and lighting are number one on registries across the U.S. With seven signature ceramic styles and patterns, the company has cornered the market for beautiful, basic, and dependable tableware. **juliska.com**

Kathryn Ireland, who designs fabrics and wallpaper sold to the trade through showrooms such as John Rosselli, has a website that sells textiles, vintage pieces, lighting, pillows, lampshades, and furniture. Her style is bright and bold, with an abundance of ikat and suzani patterns. Her website features a thorough range of her personally designed fabrics and wallpapers. **kathrynireland.com**

Lafco, located in SoHo, LA, Dallas, and Bar Harbour, distributes a number of high-end bath goods, from soap to candles. Santa Maria Novella, the Italian perfumer and soap maker, is one of their standout labels and one of my personal obsessions. One of their scented terra-cotta pomegranates in the linen closet is a life changer, as are their pomegranate bath soap, bath salts, and unisex musk shampoo. The store is a must-visit for all who take scent seriously. *285 Lafayette Street, New York, NY 10012* **lafcony.com**

Lars Bolander's Gustavian-oriented stores offer a bevy of beautiful finds, from furnishings to accessories. Though a classic Swedish aesthetic dominates, Bolander carries a range of styles and eras, both antiques and excellent reproductions, all in impeccable taste. *232 East 59th Street, Third Floor, New York, NY 10022* **larsbolander.com**

Layla. Sadly no e-commerce at this lovely, Brooklyn boutique, which stocks pashminas from Kashmir, handcrafted Indian textiles, and an amazing assortment of colorful towels in traditional terry cloth, the cotton hammer, and waffle. *86 Hoyt Street, Boerum Hill, Brooklyn, NY 11201* layla-bklyn.com

Les Indiennes has mastered the block-printed look with its range of linens and wallpaper. Playing with classic Indian motifs, Les Indiennes manipulates scale and color, rendering their designs modern and fresh feeling. lesindiennes.com

Libeco's linens are everything Belgian linens ought to be—simple, austere, and soft. Muted colors and a limited range of styles in clothing and bedding make Libeco a dependable and classic vendor of linen. Stocked at specialty stores across the U.S. and also now through Restoration Hardware. libeco.com

Liberty is renowned world wide for its fabric designs, but its vast London emporium has become the essential stopping-off point for innovative and eclectic design

in all sorts of home wares. Its Best of British series showcases new and emerging homegrown talent. liberty.co.uk

LSA, based in the U.K., produces a large range of contemporary glassware, from stemware to compotes. You want simple modern-but-elegant glasses? This is it. Style ranges from the practical to the fine. Stockists are based around the world and across the U.S. lsa-international.com

Madeline Weinrib rugs come in a large range of styles, colors, and materials, though her Eastern-influenced patterned dhurries, carpets, fabrics, and pillows are her signature. She is an artist who tweaks historical patterns to make them her own. Sold through ABC Carpet, Madeline Weinrib's products can be viewed on her website. madelineweinrib.com

Marianna Kennedy manufactures a range of home accessories, though she is perhaps best known for her colorful bead-style lamps.

The British designer sells from her shop in London and through various galleries for some of her more specialty, custom pieces. mariannakennedy.com

Marston and Langinger specializes in fine hardware, outdoor furniture, gardening supplies, and architectural structures from conservatories to pool houses. The British company's goods are available through their website. marston-and-langinger.com

Matouk's lovely linen bedding has a distinctively natural and organic look and feel. Their bed basics have a decidedly relaxed yet chic style. Matouk is sold at specialty stores throughout the U.S. matouk.com

Matteo's linens—from bedding to bath—are of the highest quality and softest hand. Simplicity and austerity best describe their aesthetic. They have a website replete with their offerings. If you like linen, you should know this company! matteohome.com

Mecox Gardens offers an extensive range of home furnishings, which the store sources from auctions and flea markets in Europe to specialty furniture designers in the U.S. They have a thorough website featuring all their wares in each of their eight shops—New York, Southampton, Palm Beach, Chicago, Dallas, Los Angeles, Houston, and East Hampton. **mecoxgardens.com**

Mitchell Gold + Bob Williams offers comfortable, affordable, modern takes on classic pieces for every part of the home. **mgbwhome.com**

Moooi's avant-garde, experimental group of designers epitomizes contemporary Dutch design. The shop is more of a gallery, displaying works from such designers as Marcel Wanders and Ross Lovegrove. *Westerstraat 187 1015 MA, Amsterdam, The Netherlands.* **moooi.com**

Moss, located in the heart of SoHo, features a delightful mix of old and new, from Sèvres porcelain to Tord Boontje lighting. Their curated selection of furniture and accessories forces you to reexamine the evolution of style. *150 Greene Street, New York, NY 10012* **mossonline.com**

Mottahedeh manufactures beautiful porcelain tableware in a range of classic and ornate styles. Lines span from Oriental to early American, and each pattern is available to view and buy on their website. **mottahedeh.com**

Nickey Kehoe, the LA-based shop curated by Todd Nickey and Amy Kehoe, abounds with midcentury-modern, industrial, and independent handmade designs. Their goods can be viewed on their website as well as on 1stdibs. *730 North Highland Avenue, Los Angeles, CA 90038* **nickeykehoe.com**

Nina Campbell's shop on London's Walton Street is the perfect place to pick out the very best of her own range of home accessories and fabrics, including lighting and stationery and complementary designs for linen, glassware and china.**ninacampbell.com**

Ochre, located in a loft-like storefront in SoHo, deftly mixes industrial and luxe with its selection of upholstery, accessories, and custom lighting. The store emphasizes handmade craftsmanship, particularly with its Canvas line of tableware. *462 Broome Street, New York, NY 10013* **ochre.net**

Oly, based in California and founded by two designers, caters to retailer and designer clientele. Their pieces are often reproductions fused with modern elements, like Louis XVI armchairs upholstered in rattan. Oly's furniture and accessories are clean, simple, and elegant. **olystudio.com**

145 Antiques specializes in, though is not limited to, nineteenth- and twentieth-century French antiques and reproductions. Love their standing lamps and Napoléon III armchairs. They have a thorough website of their inventory that includes photos and prices of their upholstery, lighting, and objets. *27 West 20th Street, #1, New York, NY 10011* **145antiques.com**

Papers and Paints is a small London-based company selling paints and wallpapers. They stock a huge range of paint colours and ranges, including historical ones, and offer a color matching service if that exact shade is still eluding you. **papers-paints.co.uk**

Paula Rubenstein's famed antique shop specializes in vintage textiles and Americana. Her collection of patchwork quilts and blankets is extensive. One can easily get lost absorbing all the objects in her small SoHo store. *65 Prince Street, New York, NY 10012*

Pierre Frey is one of the most venerable French fabric houses that is still privately owned. Their classic collection of fabrics ranges from toiles to woven textiles. They've recently started designing wallpaper as well. Their fabrics and papers are sold to the trade only. **pierrefrey.com**

Pratesi's classic Italian sheets are luxurious, elegant, and refined. Their chain embroidery is recognized the world over, and they also produce fine cashmere bedding and accessories. Their website is thorough, and they have locations across the U.S. **pratesi.com**

Quadrille/Alan Campbell's bright, sophisticated, and happy textiles and wallpapers channel preppy by way of Africa and the Caribbean. Campbell's geometric prints are lively and bold. Quadrille and Alan Campbell fabrics and wallpapers are sold to the trade only. **quadrillefabrics.com**

Ralph Lauren's cinematic eye for fashion translates to the way he designs furniture and accessories, too. His home collections revolve around themes and the idea of "lifestyle"; though his designs run the gamut of styles, he is best known in the home sphere for his deco-inspired and industrial-chic pieces. **ralphlauren.com**

Raoul Textiles, based in California, is a family-run textile company that hand-block prints its designs on Belgian linen. Their patterns range from the loosely geometric to the naïvely floral. Raoul fabrics are sold to the trade and through the John Rosselli showroom. *136 State Street, Santa Barbara, CA 93101* **raoultextiles.com**

Renee's Garden Seeds sells a wide variety of seeds for flowers, kitchen herbs, and vegetables. All varieties are available on their website, where you can find the best heirlooms, hybrids, and open pollinated varieties. The website is a great resource for gardeners of all levels. **reneesgarden.com**

Restoration Hardware, known for its elegant and relatively inexpensive bath fixtures, has recently branched out with a larger selection of furniture, accessories, and outdoor furnishings, honing a Belgian industrial aesthetic, with many pieces in reclaimed wood. **restorationhardware.com**

Robert Kime, decorator to the prince of Wales, hones his classic Anglo sensibilities, resulting in fabric, lighting, rug, and furniture lines that are rich in history, subtle, and sublime. His shop is based in London, though his fabric line is available for purchase to the trade in the John Rosselli showroom. **robertkime.com**

Roberta Roller Rabbit's bright, boisterous Indian textiles and home line of linens, rugs, tablecloths and curtains are cheerful, sweet, and well-priced. Her Upper East Side store is worth a trip, whether for beach ware or home accents. *1019 Lexington Avenue, New York, NY 10021* **robertarollerrabbit.com**

Roger Oates is the place to go if you are looking for flooring. Their wool runners, in particular, are perfect for stairs and hallways. They also offer a bespoke service if you want something more individual. **rogeroates.com**

Sarah Raven's online kitchen and garden shop is a great source of seasonal bulbs and seeds, and all types of gardening kit and accessories. Her brightly colored vessels, including pots and flower vases in glass and ceramics, are especially good. **sarahraven.com**

Schweitzer Linen makes affordable and classic bed linens and towels, many of which emulate the style of luxury brands like Pratesi. They are a reliable source for monogramming. They have a thorough website and catalog that is ill-designed but worth slogging through. **schweitzerlinen.com**

Selfridges, that colossus of a store on London's Oxford Street, houses everything from Diptyque candles to electrical gadgets for your kitchen in any funky color you might desire, with some designer exclusives, such as Diane von Furstenberg bed linens. **selfridges.com**

Society Limonta, based in Italy, sells gauzy, durable, and simple elegant linen products, from tabletop and bedding to clothing and accessories. Society is available at specialty stores throughout Europe and at ABC Home. **societylimonta.com**

Swan's Island, based in Maine, manufactures gorgeous handwoven blankets in a variety of yarns and colors. Each blanket has a signature, subtle pattern. They have a thorough website from which you can order. **swansislandblankets.com**

Tobias and the Angel design and produce their own furniture and fabrics, as well as selling a range of vintage and contemporary accessories. At Christmas their wonderful shop in Barnes, south London, becomes a veritable grotto, filled with exquisite decorations handmade from antique textiles and findings. **tobiasandtheangel.com**

Treillage, Bunny Williams's garden- and outdoor-oriented Upper East Side boutique, sells topiaries and arrangements, outdoor furniture, and antiques. It's a beautifully constructed haven well worth a trip. *418 East 75th Street and 1015 Lexington Avenue, New York, NY 10021* **bunnywilliams.com/treillage**

White Forest Pottery, designed by Nancy Bauch, features a delicate range of organic, simple pottery and tabletop items, mostly in white. Her designs celebrate the beauty of imperfect forms. **whiteforestpottery.com**

Wisteria specializes in quality reproduction furniture and accessories from various aesthetic eras. Their expansive range is stylishly conceived, and their website is reliable and thorough. Wisteria is a great resource if you are shopping for something in particular. **wisteria.com**

FEATURED DESIGNERS

These are among the designers and artists whose work most inspires me and from whom I've liberally borrowed. Thank you to each and all.

Jeffrey Bilhuber
Bilhuber and Associates
300 East 59th Street
New York, NY 10022
bilhuber.com

Peter Dunham
724 North La Cienega Blvd.
Los Angeles, CA 90069
peterdunham.com

Lisa Fine Textiles
lisafinetextiles.com

Steven Gambrel
S. R. Gambrel
55 Grove Street
New York, NY 10014
srgambrel.com

Hugo Guinness
Artist
His work can be seen at
JohnDerian.com

Albert Hadley
(Retired)
24 East 64th Street
New York, NY 10065
alberthadley.com

Nicky Haslam
NH Design
243-247 Pavilion Road
London SW1X 0BP
nh-design.co.uk

Johnson Hartig
johnsonhartig.com
ilovelibertine.com

Kathryn Ireland
9443 Venice Blvd.
Suite B
Culver City, CA 90232
kathrynireland.com

Carolina Irving
carolinairvingtextiles.com

Elliot Puckette
Artist
She is represented by
PaulKasminGallery.com

Charlotte Moss
charlottemoss.com

David Netto Design
davidnettodesign.com
Also see his articles for *The Wall Street Journal* at WSJ.com

Miles Redd
77 Bleecker Street
Suite C111
New York, NY 10012
milesredd.com

Markham Roberts
1020 Lexington Avenue
Second floor
New York, NY 10021
markhamroberts.com

Tom Scheerer
215 Park Avenue South
Suite 1701
New York, NY 10003
tomscheerer.com

Michael Smith Inc
1646 19th Street
Santa Monica, CA 90404
michaelsmithinc.com

John Stefanidis
Unit B, The Imperial Laundry
71 Warriner Gardens
London, SW11 4XW
United Kingdom
johnstefanidis.com

Temple St. Clair
Jewelry
templestclair.com

Bunny Williams
1015 Lexington Avenue
New York, NY 10021
bunnywilliams.com

GOOD BOOKS

By now you've realized that I admire a lot of dead decorators. Herewith, my favorite reads by or about great decorators, mostly dead, but also some very alive.

Billy Baldwin Decorates by Billy Baldwin (1972, Holt, Rinehart, and Winston)

The House in Good Taste by Elsie de Wolfe (2008 reissue of 1914 book, Bastion Books)

Mark Hampton on Decorating (1989, Random House)

David Hicks on Living—with Taste (1969, Macmillan Press)

David Hicks on Home Decoration (1972, Britwell Books)

Living with Design by David Hicks (1979, Littlehampton Book Services)

Living by Design: Ideas for Interiors and Gardens by John Stefanidis (1997, Weidenfeld & Nicolson)

An Island Sanctuary: A House in Greece by John Stefanidis (2010, Rizzoli)

Jacques Grange: Interiors by Pierre Passebon (2009, Flammarion)

Axel Vervoordt: Timeless Interiors by Armelle Baron and Christian Sarramon (2007, Flammarion)

Colefax and Fowler: The Best in English Interior Decoration by Chester Jones (1989, Barrie & Jenkins)

John Fowler: Prince of Decorators by Martin Wood (2007, Frances Lincoln)

Nancy Lancaster: English Country House Style by Martin Wood (2005, Frances Lincoln)

Elsie de Wolfe: A Decorative Life by Nina Campbell and Caroline Seebohm (1992, Aurum Press Ltd)

Parish Hadley: Sixty Years of American Design by Sister Parish, Albert Hadley, and Christopher Petkanas (1995, Little, Brown and Company)

TO DO

TO GET

ACKNOWLEDGMENTS

Jacob Weisberg and our children, Lily and Nathaniel, are the reason I bother about trying to make a nice home. They are the inspiration for this book, and also the whip crackers who forced it out of me. Rita Konig and Michael Specter have also sprinkled their fairy dust liberally over this project. All had more to do with this little book than any of them hoped, and I am grateful to each of them.

I still can't believe that Virginia Johnson, the crazily gifted artist and textile designer, ever agreed to do this book, and make more than two hundred illustrations in the midst of having a baby, getting married, launching a bedding collection, and running her successful fashion business. I bet now she wonders why she ever did, but fortunately for the book, it is too late. My former *domino* colleague Hilary Fitzgibbons designed this book with the sparkle, grace, and charm that is as much a feature of her personality as it is of her layouts. I will miss sitting in her kitchen working with her sweet baby gurgling beside us. I was lucky also that Maria Maggenti, a brilliant filmmaker, whom I met in a philosophy class twenty-five years ago, had a script-writing hiatus and helped me with the book.

After I published my first article, Jay Mandel of William Morris Endeavor called and offered to be my agent. It's taken fifteen years for him to get this tiny bit of payback. Aliza Fogelson, my editor at Clarkson Potter, brought this idea to me and was its patient and diligent midwife. Thanks also to Doris Cooper, editorial director of Clarkson Potter, and art director Jane Treuhaft.

And a big kiss and a hearty thank-you also to Alainna Lexie Beddie, Stella Bugbee, Sara Ruffin Costello, Stephen Fefferman, Atul Gawande, Malcolm Gladwell, Cate Hartley, Kirsten Hilgendorf, Kathleen Hobson, Charlotte Moss, David Netto, Pavia Rosati, Ben Schott, Stephen Sherrill, and Mieke Ten Have, and to my mother, Toby, who has gone on this decorating journey with me, and my father, Howard, who is happy in any house his family is in.

Make your home as comfortable
and attractive as possible
and then get on with living.

—ALBERT HADLEY